Field Guides to Finding a New Career

Human Services

The Field Guides to Finding a New Career series

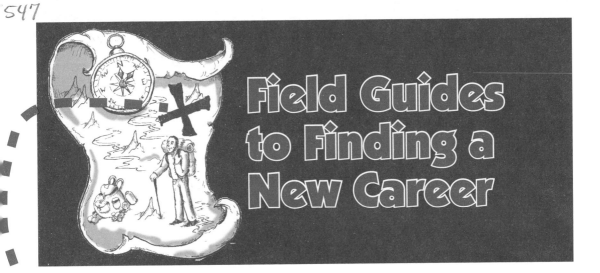

Human Services

By Scott Gillam

Ferguson Publishing
An imprint of Infobase Publishing

Field Guides to Finding a New Career: Human Services

Copyright © 2010 by Print Matters, Inc.

Ferguson
An imprint of Infobase Publishing
132 West 31st Street
New York, NY 10001

Library of Congress Cataloging-in-Publication Data

Gillam, Scott.
    Human services / by Scott Gillam.
        p. cm. — (The field guides to finding a new career series)
    Includes bibliographical references and index.
    ISBN-13: 978-0-8160-8001-4 (hardcover : alk. paper)
    ISBN-10: 0-8160-8001-1 (hardcover : alk. paper)
1. Human services—Vocational guidance.
2. Social service—Vocational guidance. I. Title.
  HV10.5.G547 2009
  361.0023—dc22
                                                                2009027907

Ferguson books are available at special discounts when purchased in bulk quantities for businesses, associations, institutions, or sales promotions. Please call our Special Sales Department in New York at (212) 967-8800 or (800) 322-8755.

You can find Ferguson on the World Wide Web at http://www.fergpubco.com

Produced by Print Matters, Inc.
Text design by A Good Thing, Inc.
Illustrations by Molly Crabapple
Cover design by Takeshi Takahashi
Cover printed by Bang Printing, Brainerd, MN
Book printed and bound by Bang Printing, Brainerd, MN
Date printed: April 2010
Printed in the United States of America

10 9 8 7 6 5 4 3 2 1

Contents

Introduction: Finding a New Career

Today, changing jobs is an accepted and normal part of life. In fact, according to the Bureau of Labor Statistics, Americans born between 1957 and 1964 held an average of 9.6 jobs from the ages of 18 to 36. The reasons for this are varied: To begin with, people live longer and healthier lives than they did in the past and accordingly have more years of active work life. However, the economy of the twenty-first century is in a state of constant and rapid change, and the workforce of the past does not always meet the needs of the future. Furthermore, fewer and fewer industries provide bonuses such as pensions and retirement health plans, which provide an incentive for staying with the same firm. Other workers experience epiphanies, spiritual growth, or various sorts of personal challenges that lead them to question the paths they have chosen.

Job instability is another prominent factor in the modern workplace. In the last five years, the United States has lost 2.6 *million jobs*; in 2005 alone, 370,000 workers were affected by mass layoffs. Moreover, because of new technology, changing labor markets, ageism, and a host of other factors, many educated, experienced professionals and skilled blue-collar workers have difficulty finding jobs in their former career tracks. Finally—and not just for women—the realities of juggling work and family life, coupled with economic necessity, often force radical revisions of career plans.

No matter how normal or accepted changing careers might be, however, the time of transition can also be a time of anxiety. Faced with the necessity of changing direction in the middle of their journey through life, many find themselves lost. Many career-changers find themselves asking questions such as: Where do I want to go from here? How do I get there? How do I prepare myself for the journey? Thankfully, the Field Guides to Finding a New Career are here to show the way. Using the language and visual style of a travel guide, we show you that reorienting yourself and reapplying your skills and knowledge to a new career is not an uphill slog, but an exciting journey of exploration. No matter whether you are in your twenties or close to retirement age, you can bravely set out to explore new paths and discover new vistas.

Though this series forms an organic whole, each volume is also designed to be a comprehensive, stand-alone, all-in-one guide to getting motivated, getting back on your feet, and getting back to work. We thoroughly discuss common issues such as going back to school, managing your household finances, putting your old skills to work in new situations, and selling yourself to potential employers. Each volume focuses on a broad career field, roughly grouped by Bureau of Labor Statistics' career clusters. Each chapter will focus on a particular career, suggesting new career paths suitable for an individual with that experience and training as well as practical issues involved in seeking and applying for a position.

Many times, the first question career-changers ask is, "Is this new path right for me?" Our self-assessment quiz, coupled with the career compasses at the beginning of each chapter, will help you to match your personal attributes to set you on the right track. Do you possess a storehouse of skilled knowledge? Are you the sort of person who puts others before yourself? Are you methodical and organized? Do you communicate effectively and clearly? Are you good at math? And how do you react to stress? All of these qualities contribute to career success—but they are not equally important in all jobs.

Many career-changers find working for themselves to be more hassle-free and rewarding than working for someone else. However, going at it alone, whether as a self-employed individual or a small-business owner, provides its own special set of challenges. Appendix A, "Going Solo: Starting Your Own Business," is designed to provide answers to many common questions and solutions to everyday problems, from income taxes to accounting to providing health insurance for yourself and your family.

For those who choose to work for someone else, how do you find a job, particularly when you have been out of the labor market for a while? Appendix B, "Outfitting Yourself for Career Success," is designed to answer these questions. It provides not only advice on résumé and self-presentation, but also the latest developments in looking for jobs, such as online resources, headhunters, and placement agencies. Additionally, it recommends how to explain an absence from the workforce to a potential employer.

Changing careers can be stressful, but it can also be a time of exciting personal growth and discovery. We hope that the Field Guides to Finding a New Career not only help you get your bearings in today's employment jungle, but set you on the path to personal fulfillment, happiness, and prosperity.

How to Use This Book

Career Compasses

Each chapter begins with a series of "career compasses" to help you get your bearings and determine if this job is right for you, based on your answers to the self-assessment quiz at the beginning of the book. Does it require a mathematical mindset? Communication skills? Organizational skills? If you're not a "people person," a job requiring you to interact with the public might not be right for you. On the other hand, your organizational skills might be just what are needed in the back office.

Destination

A brief overview, giving you an introduction to the career, briefly explaining what it is, its advantages, why it is so satisfying, its growth potential, and its income potential.

You Are Here

A self-assessment asking you to locate yourself on your journey. Are you working in a related field? Are you working in a field where some skills will transfer? Or are you doing something completely different? In each case, we suggest ways to reapply your skills, gain new ones, and launch yourself on your new career path.

Navigating the Terrain

To help you on your way, we have provided a handy map showing the stages in your journey to a new career. "Navigating the Terrain" will show you the road you need to follow to get where you are going. Since the answers are not the same for everyone and every career, we are sure to show how there are multiple ways to get to the same destination.

Organizing Your Expedition

Fleshing out "Navigating the Terrain," we give explicit directions on how to enter this new career: Decide on a destination, scout the terrain, and decide on a path that is right for you. Of course, the answers are not the same for everyone.

Landmarks

People have different needs at different ages. "Landmarks" presents advice specific to the concerns of each age demographic: early career (twenties), mid-career (thirties to forties), senior employees (fifties) and second-career starters (sixties). We address not only issues such as overcoming age discrimination, but also possible concerns of spouses and families (for instance, paying college tuition with reduced income) and keeping up with new technologies.

Essential Gear

Indispensable tips for career-changers on things such as gearing your résumé to a job in a new field, finding contacts and networking, obtaining further education and training, and how to gain experience in the new field.

Notes from the Field

Sometimes it is useful to consult with those who have gone before for insights and advice. "Notes from the Field" presents interviews with career-changers, presenting motivations and methods that you can identify with.

Further Resources

Finally, we give a list of "expedition outfitters" to provide you with further resources and trade resources.

Make the Most of Your Journey

If you investigate the jobs described in this book, you will realize that the phrase "human services" does not quite capture the spark that motivates those in this field. People in human services are usually what we call "people persons." They thrive when helping, advising, inspiring, comforting, and just being there for the wide variety of people who seek their services. Members of the helping professions—another phrase that people use to describe many of these jobs—often see their work as a calling rather than just a job. It is the human connection more than the money that moves those in the human services to do their best. It should be no surprise that caring about their clients always ranks high on the list of skills deemed important by those in this field.

One reason that people in human services care so much about the people they serve is the inspiring struggles of these clients to improve themselves. Who would not be uplifted to see a couple with serious marital problems manage to save their marriage with the help of a marriage therapist? Or to see a young man or woman, aided by a funeral service director, emerge from the trauma of an unexpected death in the family with a new appreciation of life? Or to share in the satisfaction of a client in his more efficient office, made possible in part by a professional organizer?

The lives of some of the professionals you will meet in this book are themselves inspiring. You will read about a lawyer, no longer able to practice because of a life-threatening illness, who became a successful life coach. You will encounter a young single mother of two who drove a school bus and supervised children's play groups, then transformed herself into the owner of a growing concierge business. You will meet a drug addict who decided to turn her life around and has now been counseling other addicts for over 18 years.

It might seem that the diverse occupations described in this book have little in common. After all, we are looking at professions that focus on life-cycle landmarks as distinct as marriage (marriage and family therapist); old age (retirement home manager); and death (funeral service director). Even in a series devoted to people who change careers, it would be difficult (though hardly impossible) to imagine a person changing from one of those three careers to another in the same group. Yet some of the professions in this book do share certain characteristics. Psychotherapists, life coaches, marriage and family therapists, social workers, and substance abuse counselors all try to move their clients to change (or learn to accept) some aspects of their behavior. Many social workers work in addiction treatment programs or with couples and families. Some personal assistants specialize in keeping their clients' business or personal affairs in order, as do some professional organizers. Similarly, there is some overlap between the activities of professional organizers and event planners.

Those in the human service professions, share a belief in the power of the human spirit. That spirit might be defined as the ability of ordinary people, with the help of supportive professionals, to grapple with their problems and create solutions that enable them not only to survive, but to endure. It does not follow that those in human services must be cock-eyed optimists who are naïve about the dark side of human nature. On the contrary, therapists in particular see a lot of human weakness and backsliding in their work. Yet, as a group, those in the human services would rather light a candle than curse the darkness. For them the glass is half full, and with training and patience that glass can be filled still further.

What do you need to join one of the professions in this diverse band of professional helpers? Not surprisingly, your people skills—empathy, trust, compassion—are your strongest suit for entering most of these occupations. Coming in a close second are the communication skills needed to get through to your client. These skills will help you send and receive the messages that clarify what professional and client together can do to help solve a problem. Life coaches and their clients, for example, must be clear about what each is asking the other to do in order to achieve the client's goals. People in the human services must also be able to master the relevant knowledge needed to address their clients' problems. One cannot be an effective social worker, for example, without having a firm grasp of the basic information in the field, whether it is child and foster care, adolescent psychology, job training, or gerontology. All professional helpers also help their clients create organized structures that will help give meaning to their lives. Substance abuse counselors may accomplish this goal by guiding clients through a 12-step program to treat alcoholism. Professional organizers may achieve a comparable goal in helping a client create a more organized filing system.

Before beginning your job search, asess your skills, experience, and desires. Decide whether you have the caring personality and communication and organizational skills needed to make a successful transition into a new career in human services. Then consider the educational requirements, which vary widely depending on the occupation. Working down the ladder from most requirements to least:

☞ Anybody can call himself or herself a "therapist," but in practice psychotherapists and marriage and family therapists require a doctoral degree plus clinical training.

☞ Marriage counselors and social workers qualify for their professions with a master's degree plus clinical training. All of the foregoing occupations also require a state license and in-service education.

☞ College degrees are nearly always required (or at least expected) for work as a life coach, drug counselor, retirement home manager, or event planner.

☞ Funeral service directors in some states require only a high school education plus the appropriate license, but the most successful ones have two-year or four-year degrees in mortuary science plus internships.

☞ It is possible to be a concierge or a professional organizer with just a high school education, but an increasing number have associate or college degrees.

The more education a job requires, the more you need to be sure it is the right one for you—before you make a two-or-three year commitment for a degree that qualifies you for a job that you then discover is not what you thought it would be. The best way to find out if you have a knack for jobs in which you help people is to find paid or unpaid opportunities to—you guessed it—help people. For example: Are you considering becoming a substance abuse counselor or psychotherapist? Then pursue volunteer opportunities at a local health clinic or hospital. Do you find that people often seek out your advice on practical matters involving space or time management? Then seek out informal ways to help people as a budding professional organizer or personal assistant.

Since monetary rewards are usually not a part of these opportunities, volunteering is one way to find out whether the job itself is attractive. Talking to friends who chose high-paying but stressful jobs with impossible hours may give you some perspective here. The psychic wages in human services jobs can save you thousands in doctor and psychotherapy bills resulting from stressful jobs that drain the spirit and foster cynicism and apathy. Do not let money lure you away from a job that would better allow your true passion to flourish.

You may be drawn to a particular job category because your friends find it attractive. Respect your friends' opinions, especially if you feel they know you well and have your best interests at heart. Remember, however, that you are the person who is going to be filling that job, not them. You are the only person who can make the judgment of whether it is the right job for you. Your decision to take a job should be based on your own analysis, not someone else's.

Changing careers is not always an easy task. Do not expect a job to fall in your lap by your first or second interview. Be strong in your desire and confident about your skills. Give yourself a few months or more to find your way around the job market. Ask yourself if you are prepared to consider offers that may involve long hours or a pay cut. Try to be flexible in making the decision whether to take such a job. It may be better to take a lower-paying job with long hours in a field that promises to grow and further your chances of promotion than to fall for a higher-paying position in a dead-end department. Look for support and advice from friends and professional organizations. Job-hunting is a job in itself, and as with any new venture, you should not be shy about asking for help when you need it. Fortunately, you will find many in the helping professions are as open to helping you for free as they are to helping their paying clients. Expect the prospect of changing careers to bring on some nervousness as well as excitement. That is only normal when you are entering a new field. If your nervousness far outweighs the excitement, however, then you might step back and reconsider.

To summarize, if you are thinking of changing careers and entering the broad field of human services, first consider the educational level you will need to enter the specific careers described in this book. Seek out volunteer opportunities in jobs that interest you. Listen to your friends and seek the advice of professionals in the field, but make this decision for yourself, not for them. Do not expect the transition to a new career to be quick or easy. A little nervousness is normal for anyone taking such a step. With the information in this book, however, your journey should be smoother, with fewer surprises and detours, and the final result will be a job you cannot just live *with* but live *for*. Good luck on the journey!

Self-Assessment Quiz

I: Relevant Knowledge

1. How many years of specialized training have you had?
    (a) None, it is not required
    (b) Several weeks to several months of training
    (c) A year-long course or other preparation
    (d) Years of preparation in graduate or professional school, or equivalent job experience

2. Would you consider training to obtain certification or other required credentials?
    (a) No
    (b) Yes, but only if it is legally mandated
    (c) Yes, but only if it is the industry standard
    (d) Yes, if it is helpful (even if not mandatory)

3. In terms of achieving success, how would you rate the following qualities in order from least to most important?
    (a) ability, effort, preparation
    (b) ability, preparation, effort
    (c) preparation, ability, effort
    (d) preparation, effort, ability

4. How would you feel about keeping track of current developments in your field?
    (a) I prefer a field where very little changes
    (b) If there were a trade publication, I would like to keep current with that
    (c) I would be willing to regularly recertify my credentials or learn new systems
    (d) I would be willing to aggressively keep myself up-to-date in a field that changes constantly

5. For whatever reason, you have to train a bright young successor to do your job. How quickly will he or she pick it up?
    (a) Very quickly
    (b) He or she can pick up the necessary skills on the job
    (c) With the necessary training he or she should succeed with hard work and concentration
    (d) There is going to be a long breaking-in period—there is no substitute for experience

II: Caring

1. How would you react to the following statement: "Other people are the most important thing in the world?"
    (a) No! Me first!
    (b) I do not really like other people, but I do make time for them
    (c) Yes, but you have to look out for yourself first
    (d) Yes, to such a degree that I often neglect my own well-being

2. Who of the following is the best role model?
    (a) Ayn Rand
    (b) Napoléon Bonaparte
    (c) Bill Gates
    (d) Florence Nightingale

3. How do you feel about pets?
    (a) I do not like animals at all
    (b) Dogs and cats and such are OK, but not for me
    (c) I have a pet, or I wish I did
    (d) I have several pets, and caring for them occupies significant amounts of my time

4. Which of the following sets of professions seems most appealing to you?
    (a) business leader, lawyer, entrepreneur
    (b) politician, police officer, athletic coach
    (c) teacher, religious leader, counselor
    (d) nurse, firefighter, paramedic

5. How well would you have to know someone to give them $100 in a harsh but not life-threatening circumstance? It would have to be...
    (a) ...a close family member or friend (brother or sister, best friend)
    (b) ...a more distant friend or relation (second cousin, coworkers)
    (c) ...an acquaintance (a coworker, someone from a community organization or church)
    (d) ...a complete stranger

III: Organizational Skills

1. Do you create sub-folders to further categorize the items in your "Pictures" and "Documents" folders on your computer?
    (a) No
    (b) Yes, but I do not use them consistently
    (c) Yes, and I use them consistently
    (d) Yes, and I also do so with my e-mail and music library

2. How do you keep track of your personal finances?
    (a) I do not, and I am never quite sure how much money is in my checking account
    (b) I do not really, but I always check my online banking to make sure I have money
    (c) I am generally very good about budgeting and keeping track of my expenses, but sometimes I make mistakes
    (d) I do things such as meticulously balance my checkbook, fill out Excel spreadsheets of my monthly expenses, and file my receipts

3. Do you systematically order commonly used items in your kitchen?
    (a) My kitchen is a mess
    (b) I can generally find things when I need them
    (c) A place for everything, and everything in its place
    (d) Yes, I rigorously order my kitchen and do things like alphabetize spices and herbal teas

4. How do you do your laundry?
    (a) I cram it in any old way
    (b) I separate whites and colors

(c)   I separate whites and colors, plus whether it gets dried

(d)   Not only do I separate whites and colors and drying or non-drying, I organize things by type of clothes or some other system

5.   Can you work in clutter?
(a)   Yes, in fact I feel energized by the mess
(b)   A little clutter never hurt anyone
(c)   No, it drives me insane
(d)   Not only does my workspace need to be neat, so does that of everyone around me

IV: Communication Skills

1.   Do people ask you to speak up, not mumble, or repeat yourself?
(a)   All the time
(b)   Often
(c)   Sometimes
(d)   Never

2.   How do you feel about speaking in public?
(a)   It terrifies me
(b)   I can give a speech or presentation if I have to, but it is awkward
(c)   No problem!
(d)   I frequently give lectures and addresses, and I am very good at it

3.   What's the difference between *their, they're,* and *there*?
(a)   I do not know
(b)   I know there is a difference, but I make mistakes in usage
(c)   I know the difference, but I cannot articulate it
(d)   *Their* is the third-person possessive, *they're* is a contraction for *they are,* and *there is* a deictic adverb meaning "in that place"

4.   Do you avoid writing long letters or e-mails because you are ashamed of your spelling, punctuation, and grammatical mistakes?
(a)   Yes
(b)   Yes, but I am either trying to improve or just do not care what people think

(c)   The few mistakes I make are easily overlooked

(d)   Save for the occasional typo, I do not ever make mistakes in usage

5.   Which choice best characterizes the most challenging book you are willing to read in your spare time?

(a)   I do not read

(b)   Light fiction reading such as the Harry Potter series, *The Da Vinci Code*, or mass-market paperbacks

(c)   Literary fiction or mass-market nonfiction such as history or biography

(d)   Long treatises on technical, academic, or scientific subjects

V: Mathematical Skills

1.   Do spreadsheets make you nervous?

(a)   Yes, and I do not use them at all

(b)   I can perform some simple tasks, but I feel that I should leave them to people who are better-qualified than myself

(c)   I feel that I am a better-than-average spreadsheet user

(d)   My job requires that I be very proficient with them

2.   What is the highest level math class you have ever taken?

(a)   I flunked high-school algebra

(b)   Trigonometry or pre-calculus

(c)   College calculus or statistics

(d)   Advanced college mathematics

3.   Would you rather make a presentation in words or using numbers and figures?

(a)   Definitely in words

(b)   In words, but I could throw in some simple figures and statistics if I had to

(c)   I could strike a balance between the two

(d)   Using numbers as much as possible; they are much more precise

4.   Cover the answers below with a sheet of paper, and then solve the following word problem: Mary has been legally able to vote for exactly half her life. Her husband John is three years older than she. Next year,

their son Harvey will be exactly one-quarter of John's age. How old was Mary when Harvey was born?

(a) I couldn't work out the answer

(b) 25

(c) 26

(d) 27

5. Cover the answers below with a sheet of paper, and then solve the following word problem: There are seven children on a school bus. Each child has seven book bags. Each bag has seven big cats in it. Each cat has seven kittens. How many legs are there on the bus?

(a) I couldn't work out the answer

(b) 2,415

(c) 16,821

(d) 10,990

VI: Ability to Manage Stress

1. It is the end of the working day, you have 20 minutes to finish an hour-long job, and you are scheduled to pick up your children. Your supervisor asks you why you are not finished. You:

(a) Have a panic attack

(b) Frantically redouble your efforts

(c) Calmly tell her you need more time, make arrangements to have someone else pick up the kids, and work on the project past closing time

(d) Calmly tell her that you need more time to do it right and that you have to leave, or ask if you can release this flawed version tonight

2. When you are stressed, do you tend to:

(a) Feel helpless, develop tightness in your chest, break out in cold sweats, or have other extreme, debilitating physiological symptoms?

(b) Get irritable and develop a hair-trigger temper, drink too much, obsess over the problem, or exhibit other "normal" signs of stress?

(c) Try to relax, keep your cool, and act as if there is no problem

(d) Take deep, cleansing breaths and actively try to overcome the feelings of stress

3. The last time I was so angry or frazzled that I lost my composure was:
   (a) Last week or more recently
   (b) Last month
   (c) Over a year ago
   (d) So long ago I cannot remember

4. Which of the following describes you?
   (a) Stress is a major disruption in my life, people have spoken to me about my anger management issues, or I am on medication for my anxiety and stress
   (b) I get anxious and stressed out easily
   (c) Sometimes life can be a challenge, but you have to climb that mountain!
   (d) I am generally easygoing

5. What is your ideal vacation?
   (a) I do not take vacations; I feel my work life is too demanding
   (b) I would just like to be alone, with no one bothering me
   (c) I would like to do something not too demanding, like a cruise, with friends and family
   (d) I am an adventurer; I want to do exciting (or even dangerous) things and visit foreign lands

Scoring:

For each category...

For every answer of *a*, add zero points to your score.
For every answer of *b*, add ten points to your score.
For every answer of *c*, add fifteen points to your score.
For every answer of *d*, add twenty points to your score.

The result is your percentage in that category.

Psychotherapist

Psychotherapist

Career Compasses

Survey what it takes to enter the challenging field of psychotherapy.

Relevant Knowledge of the theory and practice of psychotherapy (30%)

Communication Skills to establish and maintain trusting relationships with clients (30%)

Caring about the job is important because your clients are depending on you to help them cope with important issues in their lives like love and work (30%)

Ability to Manage Stress in order to manage patient resistance (10%)

Destination: Psychotherapist

A psychotherapist helps people who face psychological problems that keep them from getting the most out of life or even functioning on a basic day-to-day level. There are great rewards for psychotherapists who can help their clients recover a sense of joy and purpose in their lives. At a minimum, the job requires (a) the ability to diagnose the client's psychological problems; (b) empathy in helping clients confront these problems; and (c) patience and resourcefulness in dealing with the client's resistance to change. Usually a psychotherapist is a psychiatrist, psychologist, or other mental health professional who has had further training in psychotherapy. Today, however, an increasing number of psychotherapists have in-depth training in psychotherapy alone. As a result, you can call yourself a psychotherapist with as little as a two-year M.A in counseling, or as much as the seven or more years that it takes to become a psychiatrist with an M.D. who treats patients independently. In between those two extremes, you can be a psychotherapist with a three-year M.S.W., a four- to five-year Psy.D., or a five- to six-year Ph.D. There are roughly twice as many psychotherapists with master's degrees as there are those with doctorates.

Most professional associations in the field, including the American Psychoanalytic Association, have conceded that anyone can call himself or herself a psychotherapist. The American Psychology Association, however, requires that all who want to call themselves psychologists have Ph.D.s in the subject "from an organized, sequential program in a regionally accredited university or professional school."

Do any of these psychotherapists have anything in common? Surprisingly they do, though perhaps not the qualities you might think. Many people's image of the psychotherapist, reinforced by countless cartoons, is that of a somewhat aloof figure sitting silently next to a patient reclining on a couch. Psychotherapists today, however, no matter what their training or degree, are much more likely to be active participants in the therapeutic process, engaging the patient directly with questions, insights, and expressions of support.

All in all, psychotherapists are probably more different from each other than alike. The field has come a long way since Freud's demonstration of the power of talk to heal psychic wounds. While psychodynamic therapy, or talk therapies generally, enjoy popularity in the present, significantly different other approaches have taken off in the last couple generations. Humanistic psychology broke from the pathology-oriented ways of Freudianism to emphasize the positive (*self-actualization* is a humanistic term). If

Essential Gear

Diagnostic and Statistical Manual of Mental Disorders, 4th edition. Although some mental health professionals do not emphasize diagnosis, this manual (usually abbreviated DSM-IV and available both in print and online) is considered the authority in its field. Insurance companies require the numerical shorthand used in the DSM-IV for each diagnosed mental condition before they will reimburse the provider or patient.

humanistic understandings are an attempt to treat the individual holistically, cognitive behavioral therapy takes a somewhat opposite approach, seeking to identify particular views, or *schemas*, that trip a person up while providing alternative, superior lines of thinking. The fourth and last major psychotherapeutic school is systems therapy, which emphasizes the importance of relationships in a person's life. There are more than 200 documented approaches to psychotherapy, and the vast majority of practitioners would call themselves "eclectic." Many therapists also tailor their strategies to suit individual patients.

There are varied educational paths to a career in psychotherapy, but four main roads. Each requires a different advanced degree: the master's in social work (M.S.W.); the M.A. (or M.S.); the Ph.D.; and the Psy.D. A person with a master's in social work (M.S.W.) may perform psychotherapy either as an employee of a public or private agency or as an individual. Someone with an M.A. in counseling may work in specialized areas like marriage and family therapy, career or vocational counseling, or substance abuse therapy. In this role, he or she will focus on specific questions such as, "How can I improve my marriage?" or "What career should I pursue?" A specialized counselor may work under the supervision of someone with a doctorate in clinical psychology or a medical doctor (in case drugs need to be prescribed).

There are varied educational paths to a career in psychotherapy, but four main roads. Each requires a different advanced degree: the master's in social work (M.S.W.); the M.A. (or M.S.); the Ph.D.; and the Psy.D. A person with a master's in social work (M.S.W.) may perform pyscotherapy either as an employee of a public or private agency or as an individual. Someone with an M.A. in counseling may work in specialized areas like marriage and family therapy, career or vocational counseling, or substance abuse therapy. In this role, he or she will focus on specific

Essential Gear

The Interpretation of Dreams **and *On Becoming a Person.*** These two books, the first by Sigmund Freud and the second by Carl Rogers, are two classics in the field that every student considering becoming a psychotherapist will want to become familiar with. Although he was known as a psychoanalyst, not as a writer, Freud was nominated for the Nobel Prize in Literature in 1936 partly because of the clarity of his prose. Rogers's book developed the concept of client-centered therapy—the idea that the person in treatment is a client who determines the course of therapy rather than a passive patient.

questions such as, "How can I improve my marriage?" or "What career should I pursue?" A specialized counselor may work under the supervision of someone with a doctorate in clinical psychology or a medical doctor (in case drugs need to be prescribed).

A clinical psychologist has more expertise in treating individuals with potentially more serious problems like major depression or bipolar disorder. Clinical psychologists have one of two doctoral degrees: the Psy.D. (doctor of psychology) or the Ph.D. (doctor of clinical or counseling psychology). The Ph.D. gives equal emphasis to research and clinical training and takes at least six years to complete. The Psy.D. degree, on the other hand, gives more emphasis to actual clinical services such as therapy, assessment, and consultation, and less emphasis to research. The Psy.D. normally requires four to five years to finish. Both Ph.D. and Psy.D. degrees require substantial research papers and a one-year predoctoral internship.

The daily routine of a psychotherapist varies somewhat depending on the work setting. If you practice in an institutional setting like a hospital or other health care facility, you will probably work a shift that could include evenings or weekends. Those that practice in schools and clinics are more likely to work only daytime hours. Psychotherapists who have their own private practice may set their own hours, but these often include evening or weekend hours to accommodate their clients. If you work in private practice, you must seek out your own clients through advertising, networking, and referrals. Many such psychotherapists also act as their own bookkeepers and appointment secretaries. In the end, your dedication to your clients and the feeling of achievement that helping others can bring may be the most important factors in determining your success as a psychotherapist.

You Are Here

Your adventure as a psychotherapist can go in one of several directions.

Do people genuinely consider you a good listener? Having patients share their problems with you day after day demands a high degree of perseverance and empathy on your part. It also requires that you are comfortable in being yourself in the therapeutic situation instead of feeling that you are playing a role different from your true self.

How much time and money are you willing to invest in getting an advanced certificate or degree? Psychotherapists may work in one of a variety of roles, with degree requirements ranging from a two-year master's program to a full Ph.D. The master's program usually involves course work, research papers, supervised interventions with patients, and an internship. The doctoral programs have the same elements, but more extensive requirements that typically take four to seven years to complete.

Are you willing to commute or relocate in order to have a larger potential clientele for your services? Like many professionals, most mental health workers tend to cluster in the larger cities. Whole streets in New York City, for example, have been punningly described as "mental blocks" because of the number of psychiatrists and psychologists whose offices are located there. You may find a more relaxed, less competitive atmosphere in a smaller city or suburb where your services will be more in demand.

Navigating the Terrain

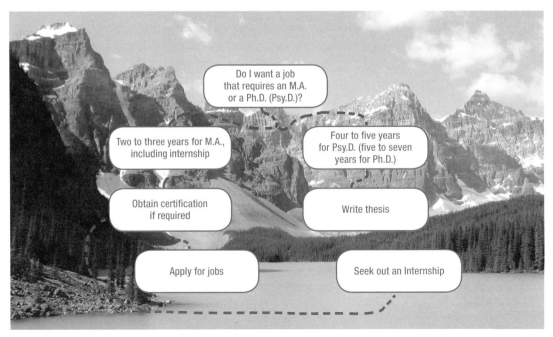

Organizing Your Expedition

Before you set out, know where you are going.

Decide on a destination. An interest in psychotherapy can lead to many possible careers, including the ones mentioned in this chapter and elsewhere in this book. You may want to consider each of these choices before gradually zeroing on the one career that seems most appealing.

Scout the terrain. If you are unsure about which kind of career in psychotherapy you want to pursue, consider taking a class in psychology or counseling to get a feel for the field. Most universities offer nonmatriculation courses in various aspects of psychology. Many famous psychotherapists were first introduced to psychology by taking such courses. Carl Rogers majored in history as an undergraduate and then entered divinity school, intending to become a minister. After taking a few courses in psychology offered at the seminary, however, he decided to become a psychologist.

Another way to investigate a career as a psychotherapist is to volunteer for a job that involves interacting closely with a client on a one-to-one basis. Examples include tutoring a child or being a counselor in a crisis center. Like psychologist Erik Erikson, who was an itinerant artist until he took a summer tutoring job, you may find you have a gift for relating to young people. Erikson's path led to a career as a child psychologist.

Find the path that's right for you. Figure out the amount of authority and autonomy you want to exercise in your career. Do you feel comfortable in being your own boss as well as the principal guide to a vulnerable person in facing life's problems? If so, you may want to aim for a Ph.D. in psychology or clinical psychology. Over one third of all psychologists (including most of those with Ph.D.s) are self-employed and therefore have almost complete autonomy in their work. If you would rather work as part of a team in which you deal with clients under the supervision of someone with a Ph.D., consider attaining an M.A. Psychology specialists with an M.A. may find work in counseling or as assistants in centers that provide mental health services. Your responsibilities will not be as great, but neither will the stresses that often come with greater responsibilities.

Notes from the Field

Larry Zelnick
Psychoanalyst in private practice
New York, New York

What were you doing before you decided to change careers?

I had been pursuing a doctorate in Ancient Semitic languages. I had hoped to teach and do research at the university level after graduation. To help support the family, I held a part-time teaching position, working with adolescents at an after-school synagogue program where teens took courses and engaged in social activities. My classes included Biblical literature and a history course in which I dressed in costume and make-up to portray characters from Jewish history.

Why did you change your career?

I was experiencing increasing frustration and waning interest my academic future. A young man of 27, I found that career goals conceived in adolescence and young adulthood were falling away. Disillusionment with some earlier held convictions were leading me to reconsider my career path. I also entered psychoanalysis at this time and considered feelings about myself and others in ways I found liberating and exciting.

At the same time, my teaching job put me in contact with inspiring colleagues and exciting and rewarding ideas about how kids learn and interact with each other. The staff with whom I taught devoted

Instead of splitting your attention between recruiting patients, treating them, and dealing with insurance companies, you can focus your main energy on treatment, which is where most psychotherapists naturally prefer to spend their time.

Landmarks

If you are in your twenties . . . If you are not dependent on full-time, paid employment for a year or more, consider volunteering in a hospital or counseling center. Here, with orientation and short-term training, you can gain valuable experience in helping individuals who are under stress.

faculty meetings to discussing the application of psychological theories of human development to the education process. I began to feel a new surge of energy and interest and sought to transform these positive experiences into professional and career opportunities.

How did you make the transition?

I enrolled in graduate courses in psychology and education and spoke with program directors at graduate schools in educational psychology, school psychology, and clinical psychology. There had recently been introduced a new degree, the Doctor of Psychology (Psy.D.), that emphasized the practitioner, clinical aspects of psychology. I decided to enroll in a doctoral program in child and school psychology. This change meant even more years of schooling, further delaying my ability to support our family financially. Fortunately, my wife took on a good deal of the financial responsibility until I was able to pull my weight.

What are the keys to success in your career?

I love my work and I feel intensely committed to the people with whom I work. It can be grueling work, with progress sometimes coming only slowly or not at all. Even so, I feel privileged to be invited into my patients' internal lives, their feelings, pain, and happiness. Without my own deeply held feelings about my patients, this career could be very difficult. I hope that it continues to be as gratifying and rewarding as it has been for the past 25 years.

Such experiences can put you in a better position when you are applying to a graduate psychology program.

If you are in your thirties or forties . . . Because you are probably older than the typical beginning graduate student in psychology, you may be a much better prospect for graduate school because of your work history and life experience, especially in jobs that have depended on your ability to cultivate therapeutic relationships.

If you are in your fifties . . . This is the period when those who have stayed in one profession typically reach their peak earning years. In an era of shrinking budgets, however, many of these high-earning positions may need to be cut or downgraded. Enter the career-changing employee who is willing to work for a lower salary. Career changers at this point in life should also remember that advanced degrees are not necessarily a prerequisite for becoming a psychotherapist. Your life experience and keen interest in helping people can count for just as much, if not more, than an extensive formal education.

If you are over sixty . . . As an older career changer, demographics may be on your side. As the baby boomer generation ages, many in this disproportionately elderly population will prefer the services of psycho-therapists closer in age to themselves.

Further Resources

The **American Counseling Association** is a 45,000-member organization that is the largest association representing counselors in various practice settings, providing support and advocacy for the profession. http://www.counseling.org

The **American Psychological Association** is the largest professional organization of psychologists in the world; its mission is to "advance the creation, communication and application of psychological knowledge to benefit society and improve people's lives."   http://www.apa.org

The **Association for Behavioral and Cognitive Therapies** is an interest group that promotes the investigation and application of behavioral and cognitive principles to a wide variety of problems.   http://www.aabt.org

Life Coach

Life Coach

Career Compasses

Examine the skills that are essential to a successful life coach.

Relevant Knowledge of the specific techniques that will encourage your client to move ahead in life (10%)

Organizational Skills to help clients reach goals within the time period they have set (25%)

Communication Skills to frame questions to help clients focus on their goals (40%)

Caring about your client's progress in setting and achieving goals (25%)

Destination: Life Coach

Life coaches work with people, usually one-to-one, to help them define and realize personal goals. According to Myles Downey, author of *Effective Coaching*, coaching is "the art and practice of inspiring, energizing, and facilitating the performance, learning, and development of the player." It is interesting that Downey uses the word "player" rather than the usual "client" or "coachee." There is no doubt that sports, where performance is the sine qua non, are an important source of inspiration for many life coaches. Some of the big names in life coaching have sports backgrounds, including John Whitmore (auto racing) and Tim Gallwey (tennis).

While psychotherapists may encourage clients to examine their past in order to achieve better self-understanding, the typical life coach focuses on changing current beliefs or behaviors that are blocking the client's achievement of goals. Since state agencies do not generally consider life coaching to be therapy, they have not sought to regulate its practice. Anybody can call himself a life coach—or, for that matter, a business coach, health coach, dating coach, or conflict management coach. As a result, there is a proliferation of coaching schools and levels and types of training. One recent study counted 273 coaching organizations worldwide and 65 different credentials.

Essential Gear

Coaching for Performance, 3rd edition (Nicholas Brealey, 2006). Sir John Whitmore's influential work has been described as the "grandfather" of coaching books. Whitmore's broad approach emphasizes the balance between life and work and his belief in the potential of every client. Whitmore's GROW model of coaching—**G**oal, **R**eality, **O**ption, **W**ill—provides a framework for a typical coaching session..

The variety of types of coaching and lack of uniform standards among the various coaching schools have led to a wide variety of courses, lengths of training time, and modes of practice. You can take a short, inexpensive coaching course online and never see a live instructor (not recommended), or you can spend thousands of dollars and hundreds of hours on classes that feature practice supervised coaching with your classmates. Reputation, cost, and quality of instruction are probably the three most important factors to take into account when choosing a program. You will need to evaluate carefully the options for coach training available where you live to determine what is most appropriate for you.

The wide range of training conditions and standards has resulted in several different coaching practices. Once they have made initial contact with their coachees, some life coaches conduct virtually all their coaching sessions by telephone, charging a flat fee for a set number of extended conversations per month. Others combine face-to-face sessions with telephone follow-up as needed. The coaching world also reflects different philosophies on how to best unlock the client's full human potential. The newer behavior-based approach, which claims to be more scientifically based and measurable, frowns upon the older and, they claim, more belief-based school of thought. Behavior-based life coaching is said to apply the techniques of behavioral science to the practice of measuring coaching performance. For example, one study compared the effect of a management training program on two otherwise identical groups, except that one group had follow-up life coaching. The study, featured in *Public Personnel Management Journal*, found that the group with life coaching showed an increase in their productivity that was almost four times as great as the group with no life coaching. Practitioners of the newer behavior-based approach call "belief-based" life coaching a "simplistic model of coaching that employs relabeled, old performance counseling strategies or, in some cases, scientifically unproven "fuzzy techniques," according to the Behavioral Coaching Institute. The belief-based approach is said to lack ways to measure its effectiveness and to depend too much on the individual personality of the coach.

Essential Gear

Co-Active Coaching: Coaching People Towards Success in Work and Life, 2nd edition (Davies-Black, 2007). This book by Whitworth, Kimsey-House, and Sandahl models the ideal coach; describes the five skills that are key to the coach's success (listening, curiosity, action and learning, and self-management); and explains the three core principles of coaching: fulfillment, balance, and process. The last section, "The Coach's Toolkit," offers detailed action plans, client activities and worksheets, and intake checklists.

According to an International Coaching Federation survey, most life-coach clients want their coaches to be both good listeners and sources of motivation. Clients may seek life coaches for a variety of reasons: relief of stress in new jobs (or after being let go from an old one); managing grief after the death of a loved one; adapting to new family situations (for example, after adopting a child or having a grown child leave home); finding new goals for a sabbatical; or simply seeking a deeper understanding of themselves and their surrounding world.

To be a successful life coach, you should also have a positive outlook on life, love people, and believe in their potential to grow. At the same time, life coaches must maintain a clear boundary between their own personal lives and those of their clients. Good coaches gently call clients' attention to their shortcomings in a nonjudgmental way and suggest specific ways in which they could improve. Since life coaches are their own bosses, it also helps considerably to have an entrepreneurial spirit and good business sense. If you are thinking of becoming a life coach, you need to examine your own life and determine in which kinds of situations you feel you can offer the most helpful insights and support. You may be able to develop a niche market that will lead to more clients and a higher visibility in the growing world of life coaching.

You Are Here

Your path to becoming a life coach starts with a genuine desire to help people succeed.

Are you a self-confident person who knows how to listen to others? Good life coaches let their coachees reveal their own goals in personal development, business, or careers. The coach provides feedback and motivation so coachees can create action plans to fulfill their dreams. The job requires the establishment of trust and respect, follow-through, and creative thinking.

Do you believe that people have the inherent ability to change? After training, the life coach is equipped to work with coachees using a variety of techniques, including mentoring, values assessment and clarification, goal-setting, and behavior modification. In the final analysis, however, it is the coachee's faith that they can achieve their goals that will be a key factor in determining how well they succeed.

Can you speak with authority when encouraging others to take new paths? Some of the best life coaches are those who have undergone trials of character and come out of the experience with hard-won insights. At the same time, it will obviously help considerably if your current life is emotionally and financially stable, so that your own needs and concerns do not intrude upon those of your coachees.

Navigating the Terrain

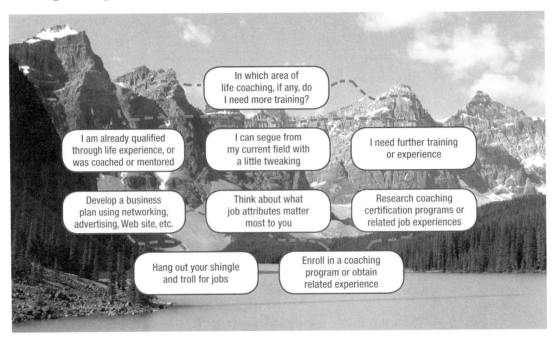

In which area of life coaching, if any, do I need more training?

I am already qualified through life experience, or was coached or mentored

I can segue from my current field with a little tweaking

I need further training or experience

Develop a business plan using networking, advertising, Web site, etc.

Think about what job attributes matter most to you

Research coaching certification programs or related job experiences

Hang out your shingle and troll for jobs

Enroll in a coaching program or obtain related experience

Organizing Your Expedition

Before you set out, know where you are going.

Decide on a destination. Life coaching is still too new a field to be recognized in mainstream academia. Therefore, individuals interested in coaching can define the job to emphasize their strengths. In this process, it is helpful to analyze your past education and experience for relevant courses and key encounters that have helped you define your goals as a coach. One successful life coach traced his interest in coaching back to his experience as a teenager caddying for business leaders on his home-town golf course. Another pointed to a course in counseling that he took as a psychology major in college. Your analysis of such factors will help you see the patterns and building blocks from which you can begin to construct your new career as a life coach.

Scout the terrain. You have essentially two options at the outset of a career as life coach. If you already have the confidence and clear vision of what you need to do to succeed, then you might start by informally counseling friends. Do not give up your day job yet, but, as word of your skills spreads, a single client may be all you need to get your business off the ground. The other path involves formal training and certification before stepping into the job market. Find out what coaching schools exist near you and how their offerings differ. Talk to some of the teachers and assess their teaching skills.

Find the path that's right for you. If you decide to go directly into life coaching, unless you are very lucky you will need to implement extensive networking, advertising, and involvement with professional life coaching associations in order to spread the word about your business. If you decide to take the educational route, realize that there is no single recognized accrediting body for life coaching. Educational preparation for this career can range from one or more courses taken at a local college to a full-year certification program offered by an established organization like the International Coaching Council or the International Coach Federation. If possible, talk to instructors and students in these courses and programs to determine which is best for you.

Landmarks

If you are in your twenties . . . Your fresh approach in the field of life coaching may well be a welcome stimulus to older persons who are in need of a new perspective. In our fast-moving and increasingly technology-driven world, as the anthropologist Margaret Mead once observed, it is often the young who teach the old rather than vice-versa, as in previous ages.

If you are in your thirties or forties . . . If you have accumulated enough life experience to observe what makes successful people tick, then a one-year life coach certification course can help you put your knowledge into action as well as give you valuable contacts that can lead you to clients.

Notes from the Field
Edward G. Modell
Professional and personal development coach
Queenstown, Maryland

What were you doing before you decided to change careers?

I was a corporate litigation attorney in private practice for 28 years. I also had taken extensive training in mediation but had not been able to develop a mediation practice due to the time demands of my litigation work.

Why did you change your career?

In 2002, I had what was sold to me as minor and minimally invasive surgery. Due to unexpected post-surgery complications, I was in hospitals for rehabilitation for two months. When I tried to return to my law practice six months later, I found that I could no longer manage the stress and intense concentration required. I was too young to retire, so I had to find a new career. The scariest part was that I never considered myself capable of doing anything else other than practicing law.

How did you make the transition?

A good friend was teaching the introductory course on life coaching at a local university and she invited me to audit her class. I enjoyed it so

If you are in your fifties . . . Having most likely reached whatever peak you are likely to have achieved in your primary career, you may now be the most psychologically ready of any age group to seek a life change. A short-term course in being a life coach could help you clarify the ways in which you can help others who are seeking similar changes in their lives, and also help you to identify even more closely with them.

If you are over sixty . . . In many ways the ideal life coach is the kind of person who has seen it all and can distill these experiences to yield nuggets of wisdom on how best to fulfill one's dreams. The sexagenarians among us are likeliest to have the most such experiences to draw on.

much that I decided to pursue certification and took a year-long training program with Coaches Training Institute (CTI). I also decided that this was an opportunity to do things differently than I did as a lawyer, and I quickly became involved in professional development and networking activities. I really liked the people I met and the mutual support that the coaching community offered. Within two years, I was president of the local chapter of the International Coach Federation (ICF) and also chaired its global regulatory committee. As an incoming member of the ICF global board of directors, one of my goals is to lead an initiative in creating good paying work for life coaches.

What are the keys to success in your career?

I remember to operate from the principles of abundance and generosity in every aspect of my life, particularly in my life coaching endeavors. Networking and marketing used to be dirty words for me. Now I see meeting new people and putting them together with one another as an opportunity to give away everything I know without expecting anything back in return. The rewards have been phenomenal, with people describing me as the "go to" person when it comes to making coaching connections in the Washington, D.C. area. I wake up every day thinking "Now what can I do today to help the world become a better place through coaching!"

Further Resources

International Coach Federation (ICF) is the largest worldwide organization for business and personal coaches. It is a nonprofit, individual membership organization. Its activities include the accreditation of coaches, operation of an independent coach referral service, and the promotion of professional standards. http://www.coachfederation.org
The **Behavioral Coaching Institute (BCI)** publishes articles and textbooks and trains coaches in 50 countries through its Master Coach certification program. Its partner, the **International Coaching Council (ICC)**, is comprised of all graduates of BCI's Certified Master Coach course. Like the ICF, the main aim of the ICC is to provide and promote behavior-based standards for validating coaching practitioners. http://www.behavioral-coaching-institute.com

Marriage and Family Therapist

Marriage and Family Therapist

Career Compasses

Know what it can take to become a successful marriage and family therapist.

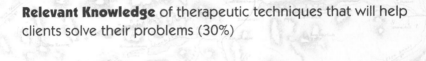

Relevant Knowledge of therapeutic techniques that will help clients solve their problems (30%)

Communication Skills so that clients can develop an action plan to improve their relationships (30%)

Caring about your clients since they have entrusted you with an important part of their lives (30%)

Ability to Manage Stress in order to manage client emotions and resistance (10%)

Destination: Marriage and Family Therapist

Marriage and family therapists (MFTs) work with individuals, couples, and families to help change individual perceptions and behaviors that cause emotional conflicts and get in the way of communication and understanding. These individuals and families may come directly to an MFT, or the foster care or criminal justice systems may refer them to an MFT. Like other therapists, MFTs use psychotherapeutic techniques and may refer some clients to a psychiatrist if necessary.

In their work, MFTs ask questions about a couple or family member's goals and the current state of their relationships. They also seek to uncover the patterns and rules that govern the interaction of the individuals involved. MFTs find that the patterns in a couple's or a family's relationships with each other can affect an individual's health condition or specific problem, which may in turn affect the couple or family dynamic. The MFT's job is three-fold: (a) point out these patterns; (b) help the individuals understand how they are affecting the problem; and (c) help individuals focus on specific actions they can take that may help to resolve the problem. Marriage therapists may work in a variety of settings, including community mental health centers, employee assistance organizations, social service agencies, courts and prisons, or in private practice. They may work flexible hours since they often deal with working couples, families, or individuals who are not available during normal business hours.

Essential Gear

The Seven Principles for Making Marriage Work (Crown, 1999). John M. Gottman and Nan Silver's text lays out the kinds of marital problems that are most common—60 percent of which are unsolvable, according to Dr. Gottman. Based on scientific research, the book describes what a couple can do to improve their marriage.

Those interested in becoming MFTs must obviously be highly motivated to help others. In their professional manner and example, MFTs should also be able to elicit respect, trust, and confidence. They should also be able to work both independently and as part of a team. MFTs must have the stamina and resilience to deal with the stress that often comes with the job. The actions of MFTs must also be in keeping with the code of ethics they agreed to abide by when they received the specific licenses and certification required in their particular state. These codes include language that defines things such as permissible relationships between clients and MFTs outside the therapist's office, circumstances under which client information can be shared with others, and the ways therapists can work with colleagues to best serve clients. In addition, the ethics codes state the obligation of therapists to recognize their own professional impairment, should it occur, and provide consultation and assistance when needed.

There are two basic paths to becoming an MFT. The first involves getting a master's degree (two to three years) or a Ph.D. (three to five years) in MFT in an accredited program. For a list of programs by state, go to http://www.aamft.org/about/coamfte/AboutCOAMFTE.asp and click on Accredited Programs. The master's degree will provide you with the basic knowledge and clinical skills, professional development, and contacts to get you started in a career as an MFT. The doctoral degree will give additional options in teaching, research, advanced clinical practice, and supervision. The second path begins with a graduate degree in a related mental health field such as psychology, clinical social work, or psychiatric nursing. You can then specialize in MFT at an accredited postgraduate degree clinical training program (see Web site listed above). In 1996 there were 75 such accredited programs throughout the United States and Canada.

After receiving their degrees, MFTs must undergo a period of about two years of supervised clinical experience before being eligible for the licensure or certification that is required in virtually all states. For information on specific state requirements, see http://www.amftrb.org. The board also administers a national licensing exam that may substitute for state licensure in some states. New laws allow insurance companies to pay many marriage therapists for their work. This development has led many marriage therapists to become self-employed and to work in either group or private practices. Other marriage therapists perform research and teach courses in their specialty.

Essential Gear

Families and Family Therapy (Harvard University Press, 1974). Salvador Minuchin's very influential work examines the family by mapping the relationships between its members and subsets. The therapist then disrupts the dysfunctional relationships within the family and tries to develop healthier patterns of behavior between family members.

The often-repeated statement that one out of every two marriages in the United States ends in divorce turns out to be false. When experts actually count the number of couples who marry and later divorce, they find two surprising statistics: (a) the divorce rate has never exceeded 41 percent; and (b) for those born since 1955, the number of divorces has actually declined slightly since 1980. The incorrect figure of 50 percent arose because researchers were comparing all the people who married in a single year with all those who divorced in that year, disregarding the fact that the two groups were composed of very few of the same people.

Despite these encouraging signs, a 41 percent divorce rate is still cause for concern. That figure is a big reason the services of marriage and family therapists not only are in demand today, but are expected to grow by 30 percent by 2016. This rate is "much faster than the average for all occupations," according to the Bureau of Labor Statistics. Many people talk about the importance of family and "family values," but marriage and family therapists are actually doing something to increase the number of couples and families that stay together. They also help those couples that do decide to divorce to form stronger relationships if they decide to remarry.

You Are Here

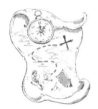

Training to become a marriage and family therapist begins with taking stock of your abilities and interests.

How comfortable do you feel about your ability to inspire respect, trust, and confidence in those you will counsel? Those who enter counseling will want to look to you as a role model for how to confront and work through their problems. Your skill in communicating your grasp of these problems will help your clients focus on the work they need to do. Your ability to encourage them to take the difficult steps necessary to change will go a long way in helping them succeed.

Can you function equally well whether working independently or as part of a team? Marriage and family therapists must often consult or work with psychiatrists, agency officials, and other MFTs in treating their clients. In dealing with others, MFTs need to be clear about the ethical implications of their actions so that they protect the client's best interests.

How specialized do I want to be as an MFT? You can be an MFT with as little as a graduate degree in the field and the passage of a state licensing exam. Or you can get a graduate degree in a related field like nursing or psychology, followed by a postgraduate degree clinical training program. The program may allow you to get specialized training in a specific area such as couples therapy.

Navigating the Terrain

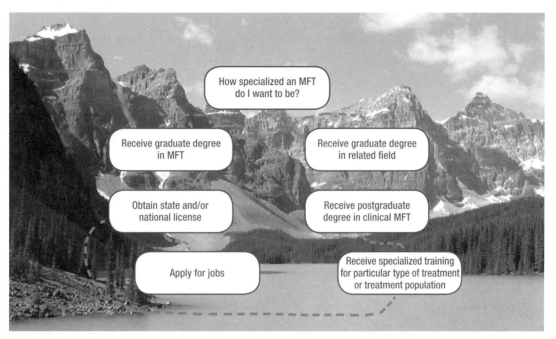

How specialized an MFT do I want to be?

Receive graduate degree in MFT

Receive graduate degree in related field

Obtain state and/or national license

Receive postgraduate degree in clinical MFT

Apply for jobs

Receive specialized training for particular type of treatment or treatment population

Organizing Your Expedition

Before you set out, know where you are going.

Decide on a destination. To make sure that marriage and family therapy is the right career for you, get some clinical experience to test your interpersonal skills and emotionally maturity. Volunteer at a women's shelter, a home for runaway teens, a crisis hotline, or a mental health center where you will have direct contact with clients. Such experience can often make up for shortcomings in your undergraduate grades. Since some MFTs conduct research and must be familiar with statistical analysis, it will be to your advantage to have courses in both research and statistics under your belt before applying for admission to an MFT program.

Scout the terrain. Consider different populations in which you feel you can be most effective: for example, families with emotional disorders, sexual abuse victims and their families, couples in crisis, those in the

Notes from the Field

Barbara A. Riggs
Marriage and family therapist
Indianapolis, Indiana

What were you doing before you decided to change careers?

I was on the faculty in a school of nursing and needed a doctorate in order to get tenure. I had gone into the Air Force right out of high school and been a medic during the Vietnam War before getting my B.S. in nursing and becoming a nurse practitioner. So my whole professional life up to that point had been in medicine.

Why did you change your career?

In the process of becoming a nurse practitioner, I had become disenchanted with the state of nursing education and the lack of empathy in the field. Because I did not want a third degree in nursing, I decided to get a Ph.D. in child and family studies, hoping that it would give me a new perspective on nursing.

How did you make the transition?

At Purdue I discovered a world outside of medicine. I went from a faculty of very cold nurses to a very warm welcome and appreciation

foster care or criminal justice systems, or young children and their parents. Also consider the settings in which you might work—including social service agencies, employee assistance programs, inpatient facilities, businesses, schools, universities, the justice system, or private practice—and decide which ones feel most appropriate for you.

Find the path that's right for you. If you are not sure whether you want a master's or a doctoral degree in MFT, consider getting a master's degree in MFT with enough counseling experience to pass a licensing test in your state. If you know MFT is the field for you but your graduate degree is not in MFT but rather a related field, find an appropriate postgraduate program in clinical MFT that will also prepare you for the licensing test.

of my background. I had always worked with families, so the new field gave me new tools to go further in helping families. When I left Purdue with my Ph.D., I went back to my old university and taught family sociology, but I found that was not where I wanted to be. So I joined a family practice where I could actually use my new skills, which I did for 15 years. During that period, I opened my own marriage and family practice and hired several other therapists. I have since sold the practice to teach a new generation of marriage and family therapists, but I continue to work at the practice part time.

What are the keys to success in your career?

The keys to my success as a marriage and family therapist are doing what I love and loving what I do. This career provides so much variety that I am never bored. When it is frustrating, I try to remember that fear is what keeps people from changing. I believe that God has given each of us the ability to be the best person we can be, and it is my job to help others to become that person.

Go back to school. As you can see from the preceding paragraph, unless you already have a graduate degree in MFT, you will have to go back to school, either for an MFT degree or for a graduate degree in clinical MFT. In deciding which schools to apply to, consider several programs before making your choice. Be honest with yourself in assessing your strengths and weaknesses and decide which school will offer you the most supported environment.

Landmarks

If you are in your twenties . . . If you do not have onerous financial responsibilities, this may be the best time to pursue your MFT credentials and get experience in working with some of the different target populations you are likely to serve.

If you are in your thirties or forties . . . If you now have family responsibilities of your own, you may want to pursue an MFT credential that will give you access to jobs with hours that will allow you more family time. You will also have a ready source of additional first-hand experience!

If you are in your fifties . . . If your other responsibilities do not permit you to take a longer route to a degree, investigate master's degree programs. Your life experience should now give you a leg up in getting admitted to graduate school. Of course, you will want to use this experience discreetly as an MFT since you need to maintain a respectful separation between your life and the lives of your clients.

If you are over sixty . . . As an elder in society, your insights into marital and family issues should now carry even more weight as you pursue an MFT degree and begin your practice.

Further Resources

The **American Association for Marriage and Family Therapy** Web site contains valuable information on graduate programs and careers in marriage counseling. http://www.aamft.org

The **American Counseling Association** Web site has a student section with extensive advice on scholarships and how to choose a graduate program. Its career center contains articles on various aspects of career planning. http://www.counseling.org

Social Worker

Social Worker

Career Compasses

Situations vary, but here is how one social worker allocated her skills mix.

Organizational Skills so that you can most efficiently manage the workflow of your practice and prioritize the needs of clients (10%)

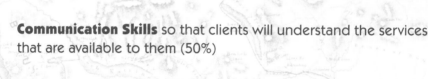

Communication Skills so that clients will understand the services that are available to them (50%)

Caring enough about clients' problems to go the extra mile to get them help (20%)

Ability to Manage Stress in the face of growing workloads, shrinking budgets, and the pressure of clients' problems (20%)

Destination: Social Worker

One way to look at the world of social work is to distinguish three types of social workers and the work they do. The first type of social worker is concerned entirely with the study of social work policy and its effect on the nation and the world. These social workers generally work for governments, universities, or think tanks. You might find them writing papers on the effects of health care policy on poor families in a particular geographical area or gauging how social workers can boost international development in Africa. The second type of social worker works with state or local agencies or small nonprofit organizations to develop programs for a particular city, town, or neighborhood. When President Barack Obama, as a recent law school graduate, worked as a community organizer in Chicago to help bring jobs to a specific neighborhood, he was practicing this type of social work. So was another prominent Chicagoan, the pioneer social worker Jane Addams, who started settlement houses for immigrants in the early 1900s and later went on to win the Nobel Peace Prize for her work as a peace activist. The third and most common type of social worker usually works with individuals and families through public or private organizations in the government or nonprofit sector.

Essential Gear

Encyclopedia of Social Work, **20th edition (National Association of Social Work/Oxford University Press, 2008).** For up-to-date coverage of the field, this four-volume set is without peer. The latest edition includes articles on demographic changes from immigration, implications of managed care, faith-based assistance, evidence-based practice, gerontology, and many other current topics.

Social workers employed by the state department of welfare or caseworkers with private charitable organizations are examples of this form of social work, as is the hospital employee assistance counselor interviewed later in this chapter.

If you are the kind of person who cares about people and who wants to improve their lives, you have probably already developed some of the skills that would make you a good social worker. For example, if you are a teacher, you may find yourself advocating for your students to the school administration. If you are a parent, you may be organizing social activities for your child and his classmates. Perhaps you find your responsibilities in the local PTA expanding to include lobbying of local politicians for more school funding. All these activities are signs of a potential social worker in the making.

Individuals and families who approach social workers for help may need a variety of services, including medical care, financial assistance, and vocational rehabilitation. Your interest in these kinds of services and your ability to master information in such fields will go a long way toward making you an effective social worker. If you find yourself drawn to newspaper and magazine articles on such topics as welfare policy, job training, family dynamics, or child care, just to take a few examples, then you are already on a track that could lead you to social work.

Equally important in social work as a profession will be your ability to explain information to a wide variety of people. Communication skills are valuable in any kind of job, but especially so in a field like social work where you must serve the different needs of people from many social and ethnic backgrounds. If you are now in a field like teaching or customer service where you communicate directly with the public, then you already have a leg up on this aspect of social work that will serve you well when you decide to change careers.

It may make some people uncomfortable to contemplate, but some professions flourish in times of adversity. During the Great Depression, union organizers and social workers sought help for unemployed workers and the one-third of a nation that, in the words of President Franklin Delano Roosevelt, was "illhoused, ill-clad, ill-nourished."

Essential Gear

Social Work Career Development: A Handbook for Job Hunting and Career Planning **(National Association of Social Workers, 2005).** For practical advice on finding a career in social work, Carol Nesslein Doelling's guidebook is made to order. In addition to a comprehensive view of job functions, fields, and degree levels in social work, it contains self-assessment exercises and up-to-date information on strategies for researching the job market, tips on selecting graduate programs, and more.

Today, as the current economic downturn threatens to become severe, you can be sure that more people will again turn to social workers for help. As a newly minted social worker, you have important role models from the 1930s in social workers like Frances Perkins, who became the first woman to head the U.S. Department of Labor, and Harry Hopkins, who rose to become the head of the federal Works Progress Administration (WPA), the nation's largest employer during the 1930s.

To practice social work, you must have a minimum of a bachelor's degree, and often an advanced degree. In addition, all states require that that you either register or take an exam in order to be licensed or certified. In New York, for example, most social workers are either a licensed master social worker (LMSW) or a licensed clinical social worker (LCSW). The two degrees are essentially the same except that the LCSW allows the practitioner to do psychotherapy and make clinical diagnoses. In many states, social workers are required to take continuing education courses to maintain their licenses or certification.

You Are Here

Take stock of your potential to be a successful social worker.

Do you want to help people to make life better for themselves, their families, and society? Social workers can improve peoples' lives in a variety of settings, ranging from public agencies to private practices. For example, you may help a recently widowed senior citizen deal with depression over the loss of his spouse by encouraging him to come to the local senior center and find companionship. Many social workers also work for social change by advocating for policies in such areas as law enforcement, health care, and equal opportunity.

Do you consider yourself emotionally mature and clear-eyed when facing difficult human problems? Your ability to remain balanced, focused, and caring, even when your clients show extreme emotional dis-

Navigating the Terrain

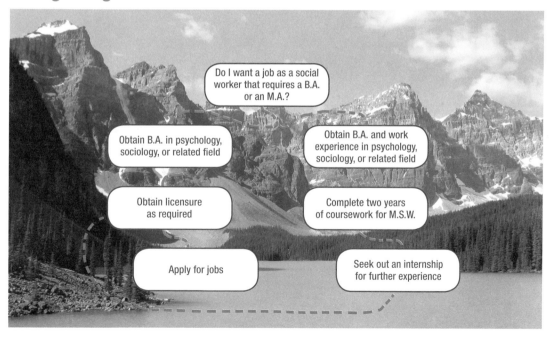

Do I want a job as a social worker that requires a B.A. or an M.A.?

Obtain B.A. in psychology, sociology, or related field

Obtain B.A. and work experience in psychology, sociology, or related field

Obtain licensure as required

Complete two years of coursework for M.S.W.

Apply for jobs

Seek out an internship for further experience

tress, will be one factor in your success. You may be called to a home where the parents of two young children have just been arrested for a drug-related crime. You must be able to explain to the children what has happened, find a suitable home for them while their parents are unavailable, and calm their fears about the situation.

Can you explain information, elicit understanding, and enlist clients' cooperation in helping them to solve their problems? Your ability in these areas will play a significant role in determining a successful outcome. As a social worker for a public welfare agency, for example, you may explain to a young mother whose husband has just deserted her how she may qualify for public assistance. You may gain the client's confidence by explaining in simple terms the sometimes complex steps that must be followed to receive welfare. You may enlist clients' cooperation by expressing concern for her situation and stressing how taking these steps will help her better care for her child.

Organizing Your Expedition

Before you begin your adventure in social work, do a little research and planning.

Decide on a destination. Do some research to consider in which of the many areas of social work you might feel most comfortable working. These areas include public welfare agencies, departments of justice and corrections, schools, mental health clinics, employee assistance programs, and rehabilitation facilities, among others. Also consider social work in related careers such as a marriage and family counselor or as a substance abuse counselor.

Scout the terrain. With over a half a million social workers employed nationwide, chances are that you know someone who can at least refer you to someone in the social work field. Talk to a social worker about his or her job. If possible, arrange to shadow that person on the job to get an idea of what a day in the life of a social worker is really like. Ask for references to social workers with different specialties who can give you a wider sense of possibilities in the field.

Go back to school. Your bachelor's degree may well qualify you for some jobs, especially in rural areas. Nevertheless, an M.S.W. is increasingly the requirement for many positions, especially in metropolitan areas. In acquiring an M.S.W. you also have the opportunity to develop a network of professional contacts. You can cultivate such contacts while taking courses and volunteering for student activities. These contacts can prove invaluable when you need a recommendation to accompany your applications for internships, which can sometimes lead to fulltime jobs. If you can afford the time and money, your investment in a master's degree will pay off in increased opportunities and bigger paychecks. According to the Bureau of Labor Statistics, the market for social workers is expected to increase over 20 percent by 2016—a much faster increase than the average for all occupations.

Landmarks

If you are in your twenties . . . If you do not have other major commitments at this point in your life, you could profitably use this time to read, take courses, and volunteer in fields that will help you gain practical insights into how you can help others better cope with the problems of life.

If you are in your thirties or forties . . . At this stage, you have hopefully established solid relationships in work and life. As a social worker, you can use the insights you have gained as a more mature person not only to make the best use of your time in graduate school but also to better help the clients you will encounter in internships.

If you are in your fifties . . . If you have come this far in life, even if you do not have children of your own, you are likely to be more concerned with how you can help meet the needs of the next generation. This attitude will give you a useful perspective and motivation as a social worker.

If you are over sixty . . . If you have the courage to change careers at this point in your life, chances are that you can encourage in others as well the kind of risk-taking that is necessary to bring about change in their lives.

Notes from the Field

Myrla Van Sluytman Parrish
Employee assistance counselor
New York, New York

What were you doing before you decided to change careers?

I was a marketing manager in cosmetics for a major company. I worked there for 10 years and two years before that at another firm, as well as in some sales positions along the way.

Why did you change your career?

After a certain number of years, marketing was not as satisfying. It was a very numbers-driven business, with a lot of report writing, and after a while I just did not care enough about it to do it as well as I had in the past. I tried different ways to stay within the marketing field, because the money was very good. My company would have paid me to get an MBA, but I just was not interested enough. As a child it had been my dream to be a psychoanalyst. In sixth grade I had a very difficult teacher, and I wondered how she had gotten to be so mean. But I knew nothing about social work as a profession. I had always enjoyed helping people and counseling friends. My ex-husband is a social worker and so I was exposed in that way to the field.

Further Resources

The **National Association of Social Workers** is the largest professional organization of social workers in the world, with 150,000 members. NASW promotes the professional growth and development of its members, sets and maintains professional standards, and advocates for sound social policies.   http://www.socialworkers.org

The **Council on Social Work Education** lists accredited social work programs at universities in the United States.   http://www.cswe.org

How did you make the transition?

While I was still working in the corporate world, I decided to take a nonmatriculation course in social work policy at Hunter College School of Social Work. I got an A and was encouraged to continue. At the same time, my company was planning to downsize. I actually "volunteered" to be let go, received a severance package, and soon thereafter I started social work school full time.

What are the keys to success in your career?

One thing I have learned about social work is the importance of networking. Every interview I have ever gotten in this field is through people I know. The path to an M.S.W. normally involves unpaid internships during your first and second year, and these internships can be a valuable source of contacts. As a student I was also involved in the school curriculum committee, which gave me exposure to the faculty and deans. I was one of four candidates for my current job, and I was told it was my marketing experience that made the difference in my being hired. Part of my job is to market our services to smaller organizations that cannot afford to have their own employee assistance programs.

Substance Abuse Counselor

Substance Abuse Counselor

Career Compasses

Set your sights on becoming an effective substance abuse counselor.

Relevant Knowledge of the techniques of successful counseling (30%)

Communication Skills to gain the client's commitment to change (25%)

Caring that leads to a trusting relationship with your clients (25%)

Ability to Manage Stress in the face of clients' resistance to change (20%)

Destination: Substance Abuse Counselor

A substance abuse counselor has an important, challenging, and personally rewarding job that can literally save lives. It is also a job much in demand today. Even though drug use overall has declined in the last several years, only a small percentage of those needing treatment are actually getting it. To help meet the challenges of treating substance abusers, counselors combine an inherently optimistic view of the patient's ability to change with an arsenal of treatment interventions to help bring about that change.

The job can be very gratifying as counselors help people successfully turn their lives around. Indeed, some of the most effective substance abuse counselors are former addicts who have transformed their own lives.

If you are patient and tolerant of what society generally regards as unacceptable behavior, you could already be well along a career path if you choose this occupation. Ideally, as a prospective counselor you enjoy the challenge of working with difficult patients. You must be able to engage them while still maintaining clear boundaries between your life and theirs. You also should have a realistic view of the patient's ability to change, and you must respect the patient's basic autonomy.

Essential Gear

Substance Abuse Counseling: Theory and Practice, 3rd edition (Pearson, 2004). For a comprehensive approach to the subject, this is a good place to start. The book includes the history of the field; basic terminology; case studies; descriptions of major addictive drugs; diagnosis; methods and steps in treatment, prevention, and intervention with selected cultures and specific groups, such as the elderly and those with disabilities; and latest research findings.

The current results of the nation's "war on drugs" are encouraging, but mixed. Use of all drugs among youth from 12 to 17 has dropped over 2 percent in recent years. Among young adults, ages 18 to 25, historically the group with the highest rates of substance abuse, between 2006 and 2007 cocaine use dropped 23 percent while and methamphetamine use decreased 33 percent. However, nonmedical use of prescription pain relievers increased in 2007 among young adults, as did illicit drug use in general among those 55 to 59. There is still much work to do, and not nearly enough substance abuse counselors to do it. By 2016 the Bureau of Labor Statistics estimates that demand for counselors in this general area will increase by 34 percent—much faster than the average for all occupations. If we assume that the economic recession that began in 2007 continues, it is likely that the demand for more substance abuse counselors will increase still further as society's levels of general anxiety and psychological depression rise significantly.

Substance abuse counselors must also deal with the perception of many people, including some drug addicts themselves, that drug abuse is simply the result of weak moral character or lack of willpower. As all substance abuse counselors are aware, the truth is that while poor choices may play a role, substance addiction itself is a real physical disease that professionals can successfully treat with a combination of medical and psychological interventions. The supportive but realistic attitude of the counselor is essential in facilitating the patient's recovery.

The substance abuse counselor uses a variety of techniques to lead patients to confront their illness. The first step is to persuade the patient to enter treatment (or in some cases to commit the patient involuntarily). To accomplish this goal, the counselor may provide information, challenge the patient's denial of the problem, and point out self-destructive behaviors, keeping in mind that the patient may have psychiatric as well as physical symptoms. Once the acute symptoms of the illness(es) have been stabilized, counselors focus on helping recovering addicts cope with the desire to return to drugs by encouraging abstinence, noting progress in treatment, and persuading patients to join self-help groups where they can work on recovery issues. With the counselor's help, patients begin to build a new structure in their lives that does not revolve around drugs. These initial phases of treatment may last up to three months.

Essential Gear

Treatment Improvements Protocols. Both the Substance Abuse and Mental Health Services Administration and the Center for Substance Abuse Treatment (SAMHSA/CSAT) publish more than 40 free, Web-based reports containing Treatment Improvement Protocols (TIPS) on many aspects of substance abuse, such as how to screen for infectious diseases among substance abusers and the differences between treating adolescents and adults for substance abuse. http://www.ncbi.nlm.nih.gov/books/bv .fcgi?rid=hstat5.part.22441

As recovery progresses, counselors help patients cope with negative feelings like anger, depression, and anxiety. During this phase, which may last up to eight months, counselors usually work with medical doctors, who may prescribe drugs to help manage negative feelings. As these feelings subside, doctors may taper off medication. In the last phase of recovery, counselors help patients to continue to work with lingering symptoms through counseling and support groups. As part of a team that may include a psychiatrist, psychologist, nurse, and other professionals, as well as a support group of peers, the substance abuse counselor plays a vital role as an agent of change in the lives of substance abusers.

Because the demand for drug counselors far exceeds the supply, it is possible to enter the field with as little as a bachelor's degree and some experience as a volunteer in a counseling setting. In some cases, according the Bureau of Labor Statistics, you may only need a high school diploma and certification to become a substance abuse counselor. Those that stay in the field, however, eventually seek both certification and licensure, the requirements for which vary widely from state to state.

You Are Here

You can become a substance abuse counselor from several different places.

Are you the kind of person who can take a sympathetic, supportive, and nonjudgmental attitude toward a substance abuser, no matter how dire the situation? If you are a person with a firm belief that addicts are victims of a treatable disease rather than people who just lack willpower, your convictions can carry you far in this field. Probably the most common potential conflict that arises between counselor and substance abuser is when the abuser at some point denies being an addict in spite of evidence to the contrary presented by the counselor.

Do you have a bachelor's degree plus some counseling experience in a related field or the equivalent life experience? This life experience could include volunteer work in a crisis center, courses in a related field, or your personal experience as a former addict. Because the demand for substance abuse counselors is so great, you may not need certification. Keep in mind, however, that job requirements may become stricter if funding cutbacks make positions scarcer.

Are you ambitious enough to seek an M.A., M.S., or M.S.W. and then pursue certification in substance abuse counseling? If so, you could be on track to assume a supervisory role in treating those who are chemically dependent. By removing you from most daily contact with addicts, being a supervisor may have the advantage of lowering your stress level, though a good supervisor is always aware of the problems faced by his clients. The higher salaries that go with advanced degrees can also cushion your stress level by affording you the means to take longer vacations for rest and recuperation.

Navigating the Terrain

Do I want a job that requires a B.A. or an M.A.?

Obtain B.A. as an end degree

Obtain B.A. on way to M.A.

Obtain state certification as needed

Complete two to three years of schooling

Apply for jobs

Receive M.A. in counseling or related field

Organizing Your Expedition

Before you set out, know where you are going.

Decide on a destination. The Substance Abuse and Mental Health Administration of the U.S. Department of Health and Human Services sponsors the Substance Abuse Treatment Facility Locator (http://find-treatment.samhsa.gov). The locator lists over 11,000 treatment facilities, including residential and outpatient programs and hospital in-patient programs that specialize in drug addiction and alcoholism. Check out this site to find treatment centers in your area. Offer to volunteer at one such center in order to gain experience in as many aspects of the organization as you can, including intake, case management, group education, and counseling. Your observations will help you decide in which areas you can best use your skills and interests.

Scout the terrain. Be inspired by listening to the testimonials of individuals with various responsibilities in treating substance abuse, includ-

Notes from the Field

M.W. Ledum
Substance abuse counselor
Portland, Oregon

What were you doing before you decided to change careers?

I had been teaching for 5 1/2 years in a Montessori school. I loved teaching. There was pure joy in watching the face of a child when she grasped a new idea or wrote her name for the first time. What I did not like was the politics of teaching, interstaff conflicts, the snail pace of administration, and parents who were often disconnected from their children.

Why did you change your career?

I was terminated by my last employer when it became known that I was a lesbian. I had no desire to work in a field where "if they find out." is a constant undercurrent. I had also become discouraged with the American education system, which I believe is more about teaching what to think rather than how to think. I was looking for an opportunity to continue being a part of change and growth in peoples' lives, but

ing counselors, educators, and administrators. You will find their stories on http://www.Addictioncareers.org in a video called "Imagine Who You Could Save." Browse Web sites like http://www.attcnetwork.org/degrees/search.asp to find a list of eleven professionals in the field of substance addiction who have volunteered to answer by email your questions about the profession.

Find the path that's right for you. Talk face-to-face to professional substance abuse counselors who work in different kinds of organizations. Discover how each job differs in daily responsibilities. Ask how much experience the counselors have had in this field, and what they like and dislike about their job. Find out what other jobs they may have had in this field, and what advice they can offer to you. Their experiences will give you a valuable first-hand perspective from inside the world of substance abuse treatment.

in a different way. By this time I had been clean and sober for about five or six years, and working in treatment seemed like an avenue to explore.

How did you make the transition?

I started out in a residential facility on the support staff–basically a "baby sitter." I attended all the training sessions I could and soon was promoted to an entry level counseling position in an outpatient program. I kept pursuing more advanced positions and was eventually certified. Over the past 18 years I have worked with adolescents, the homeless, female offenders, rural and urban populations, the poor, the mentally ill, and I have loved it all.

What are the keys to success in your career?

I think the primary reason is the strong desire to be a part of positive change in peoples' lives. I know that I cannot change anyone by myself, but I can help them change if they are willing. I love my job. That does not mean every day is great, but every day I get the chance to help make the world a better place for at least one person, one family, one community.

Go back to school. The Addiction Technology Transfer Center Network (http://www.attcnetwork.org) offers a wealth of information through their 14 regional centers, online resource library, calendar of on-site short-term education courses, and more. The site also highlights an online book club that features books by and about recovering addicts. A cross-reference to a related site, www.AddictionEd.org, lists online courses in addiction treatment. To find out if you are a suitable candidate for such distance learning courses, go to http://www.e-Learners.com and answer their questionnaire.

Landmarks

If you are in your twenties . . . A course in substance abuse counseling will add to your natural advantage as a twenty-something, since adolescents and young adults—the age group most vulnerable to substance abuse—are also the most likely to identify with a counselor in your age bracket.

If you are in your thirties or forties . . . Turnover in substance abuse counseling can be high because of budgetary constraints on wages and the stresses of the job. This situation could make your life experience and training as a counselor more attractive to employers if you also bring to the profession some related job experience and a supportive attitude.

If you are in your fifties . . . Some substance abusers may respond more positively to those they regard as father or mother figures. Your lack of experience as a new drug counselor may not be as important as your ability to command some respect because of your age. A background in any of the other branches of the counseling profession—school, vocational, rehabilitation, marriage and family, multicultural, and mental health—could provide a good foundation for a segue into drug abuse counseling.

If you are over sixty . . . Even though you are coming into the profession relatively late, your accumulated life experience can stand you in good stead. Having come to this point in life still believing in the possibility of personal change, you can be a model of ego integrity for substance abusers who are fighting to overcome negative feelings.

Further Resources

The **National Institute on Drug Abuse** conducts research on drug abuse and addition and disseminates and uses the results of that research to improve prevention, treatment, and policy as it relates to drug abuse and addiction. Their Web site contains a wealth of scientifically tested information on all aspects of this problem.   http://www.nida.nih.gov

The **Drug Abuse Treatment Outcomes** Web site summarizes the effectiveness of various treatments, based on studies done with various substances and various populations during the 1990s. These studies were originally published in 85 different sources. While some of the material requires PowerPoint software to download, the great majority of the material is only a click away.   http://www.datos.org

Funeral Service Director

Funeral Service Director

Career Compasses

Get your bearings on these skills needed by a funeral service director.

Organizational Skills to coordinate multiple steps and tight schedules (25%)

Relevant Knowledge of the scientific and business aspects of a funeral service enterprise (25%)

Caring for the families of the deceased in their time of grief (30%)

Ability to Manage Stress in order to deal with unpredictable work schedules, looming deadlines, and difficult emotional situations (20%)

Destination: Funeral Service Director

If there was ever a job where first-hand experience trumps book learning, this is it. Almost every funeral service director will tell you to try out this job before committing valuable resources to a career for which you may not be temperamentally suited. Let's face it: death is not a subject that many people feel comfortable even talking about, let alone facing directly on a daily basis. Many people try to take a humorous approach. Poet Lawrence Ferlinghetti chuckles ironically at the "smiling mortician"

who strolls by just when you are "living it up." Woody Allen jokes that he is not afraid of death—he just doesn't want to be there when it happens. Underneath the humor, however, a death in the family remains a serious matter that can engulf unprepared loved ones of the departed in a downward spiral of grief and sadness.

Enter the funeral service director with comforting words of understanding and support. The director supervises or personally accomplishes both the removal of the body of the deceased from the place of death and the preparation of the body for burial. The director also helps plan funerals and memorial services that may include prayer, music, and shared memories of the departed. The elements of a funeral or memorial service are as varied as the beliefs and practices of the mourning relatives who may help plan the event. The funeral service director needs to be tolerant of the ways in which people of different religions and backgrounds express their feelings and beliefs.

Essential Gear

How to Be a Funeral Director. This is a Web site that offers a succinct and realistic introduction to this career. A series of well-produced and substantial online videos show several aspects of a funeral director's life, including meeting with the deceased's relatives, embalming, and cremation. http://www.squidoo .com/howtobeafuneraldirector

The funeral director not only provides emotional support for the bereaved but also deals with practical matters like filing death certificates and claims for death benefits and helping the family choose a casket or urn for the remains. Have you experienced the death of a loved one? Did you find it helpful to grieve and to comfort others who grieve? Do you enjoy helping others? Do you believe it is important to be involved in your community? Are you interested in the human biological sciences? Do you have good business sense? If you answered yes to these questions, you could be a candidate for a career as a funeral service director. Keep in mind that this is not a 9 to 5 kind of job. Grieving family members may call you at odd hours, and the sooner you respond, the easier the body is to prepare for embalming, if that is the choice of the survivors. You must also attend to the survivors' needs, which may include preparing an obituary for the local newspaper under deadline. You will need organizational skills to coordinate your roles, whether as mortician, embalmer, service planner, business manager, or any combination of these.

Once you have made the basic decision to pursue this career, decide whether to include embalming as part of your job description. Some funeral homes split the responsibilities between funeral director and embalmer, but most do both. Either way, you are responsible for carrying out the family's wishes. Projections for 2010 are that upwards of 38 percent of all deceased in the United States will be cremated, with the figure rising to 51 percent by 2025, according to the National Funeral Directors Association. Here is another statistic to ponder: Beginning in 2010, the U.S. Bureau of the Census expects the death rate in the United States to rise over 32 percent, from 8.9 to 13.7 per 1,000. In short, the funeral service industry, which has always been a steady source of employment, will soon become a high-growth industry. It may be eye-opening to point out that, unlike in the past, over half the graduates of mortuary science programs today are women.

Essential Gear

American Funeral Directors Association. Check out the Web site of this organization at http://www.afda.org. Click *About Funeral Service* on the home page to go to the *Funeral Career Center.* Here you will find valuable information on mortuary science programs, state funeral service associations, scholarships, licensing boards, B.A. completion programs, and continuing education.

If you have worked in a funeral home or the morgue of a local hospital, and it has been a positive experience, you are ready to tackle the "book learning" that is also required of a future funeral director. You may choose between a two- or four-year program in mortuary science at any of around 50 colleges nationwide. Here your courses will include anatomy, pathology, embalming techniques, business and accounting, and client services. You will also take courses in the social sciences like psychology, grief counseling, funeral service law, and ethics. Most states require a one-year apprenticeship and the passage of a qualifying exam in order to get a license. Contact your state licensing board to find out their specific requirements.

A career as a funeral service director may not be for everyone, but those who have stayed in the profession find it both emotionally and materially rewarding. Like the obstetricians who bring most of us into the world and the religious leaders who marry us, the funeral service directors who bury us are respected pillars of the communities they serve.

You Are Here

You can become a funeral director from several different locales.

Are you comfortable being around the deceased? You can find out by volunteering or working in a local funeral home or hospital morgue. While most of us rarely if ever see a dead body, in a funeral home you could be face to face with one at any time of the day or night.

How much time and money are you willing to invest in getting the courses or degree(s) and license required to practice? In some states, all it takes is a high school or GED diploma and a license to be a funeral director (though not an embalmer). In other states you will need an associate degree, a B.A. (or the equivalent), or even an A.A. *and* a B.A., as well as a license.

Navigating the Terrain

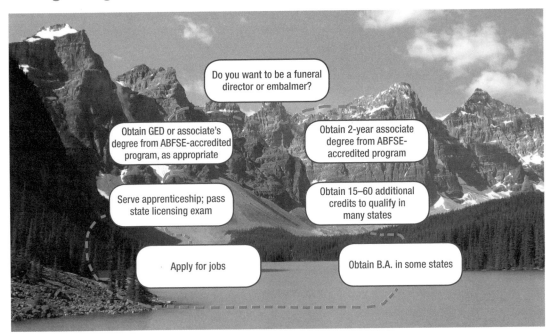

Do you want to be a funeral director or embalmer?

Obtain GED or associate's degree from ABFSE-accredited program, as appropriate

Obtain 2-year associate degree from ABFSE-accredited program

Serve apprenticeship; pass state licensing exam

Obtain 15–60 additional credits to qualify in many states

Apply for jobs

Obtain B.A. in some states

Notes from the Field
Theresa Correa
Funeral director/Arrangement director
Las Vegas, Nevada

What were you doing before you decided to change careers?

I worked in telecommunications sales, sales management and operations/ technical management for 11 ½ years, and later was in sales and marketing for two manufacturing companies. I also did a lot of volunteer work and found my passion with the Lucent Telephone Pioneers, a volunteer organization and service club made up of telecommunications industry employees and retirees.

Why did you change your career?

I wanted to get into a career that was less corporate driven and one that was more self-fulfilling. Volunteer and nonprofit work provided me with a more global sense of purpose. I realized we are all here to make a positive difference for other people.

How did you make the transition?

I did a lot of research on different careers, positions, and industries to narrow down possible career paths. Then I decided to take a part-time

How flexible are you in the hours you are willing to work and your job location? Death does not always arrive in a timely fashion. In smaller establishments you may be on call at all hours. Jobs are often more plentiful in less populated areas. Are you willing to work in places that might not be your first choice?

Organizing Your Expedition

Before you set out, know where you are going.

Decide on a destination. Your choices in this occupation are relatively simple. You can decide to be a funeral director, a funeral director/ embalmer, or an embalmer. Smaller establishments are likely to want

position at a funeral home while continuing to work full time. I quickly discovered funeral service is where my passion and talents would be best served. I sold my house, got a scholarship to mortuary school, moved across the county, and enrolled in a mortuary science program at an accredited college. After graduating and passing the national board exam, I moved back to Iowa to complete my internship and become licensed as a funeral director and embalmer. From there, I was offered a position at a Palm Mortuary in Las Vegas. I love my job.

What are the keys to success in your career?

Death is the hardest thing a family will ever have to go through. Helping them is a privilege and it gives me a feeling of gratification. I try to keep a positive outlook, always look for the good in people, try to have patience, and work very, very, very hard while also being proactive. I try to keep learning every day, remember to have fun, laugh often, and surround myself with supportive family and friends, especially my husband and mother. A huge part of my success is the people I work with every day. Good values and a strong faith keep me going when things get tough. I never give up and remember to put myself in the other person's shoes to get a fresh perspective.

candidates who combine both roles. Larger establishments may prefer those who specialize in one role or the other. Reading career literature provided by the National Funeral Directors Association is one way to help you determine in which area you are most likely to succeed.

Scout the terrain. Volunteering or working in some capacity at a funeral parlor is the best way to find out where your preferences and strengths lie. Auditing one or more courses at a local college or university that offers courses or degrees in mortuary science may also help you decide which aspect of the profession best suits you. Consider courses that assess not only your "people skills" but also your business, scientific, and esthetic skills. The best funeral directors are those who can plan and stay on schedule, yet are flexible enough to react quickly and appropriately to the inevitable surprises in doing their jobs.

Find the path that's right for you. The funeral director without embalming expertise must still feel comfortable working around the dead. Conversely, those who specialize in embalming must have the esthetic sense to prepare the body in a way that meets both the scientific standards of mortuary science and the personal standards of the family of the deceased. Either way, volunteering in a funeral parlor or serving an actual apprenticeship is the best way to decide which path is right for you.

Go back to school. No matter which of the three choices you make, the chances are almost 100 percent that you will require additional schooling. This will most likely consist of a two-year associate degree from a program accredited by the American Board of Funeral Service Education, plus successful passage of a licensing exam. Even after you are hired as a funeral director, more than 30 states require continuing education if you are to maintain your license.

Landmarks

If you are in your twenties . . . As a younger person you are more likely to have the energy and stamina to adapt to the irregular hours and stresses that can weigh more heavily on older employees. Network with older neighbors to find out which local funeral homes are likely to welcome career-changers. Make contacts with these places, and also investigate educational opportunities in mortuary science.

If you are in your thirties or forties . . . Try volunteering for experience or actually serving a formal apprenticeship that may count for credit when you go for your associate's degree. If you have the right "people skills" to convey a sympathetic, supportive attitude, these qualities will be recognized and you may well be on the road to a new career path.

If you are in your fifties . . . Recognize that a career change at this stage in your life may involve a sacrifice in terms of your family life and financial resources. Against that, however, you should weigh the value that your greater life experience will have in the eyes of your clients.

If you are over sixty . . . According to the Bureau of Labor Statistics in 2006, "Funeral directors are older, on average, than workers in other occupations and are expected to retire in greater numbers over the coming decade." This may be the best time to take the educational steps to become a funeral director, since clients will expect you to have a greater store of life experience.

Further Resources

The **American Board of Funeral Service Education** is the sole nationally recognized accreditation agency for college and university programs in funeral service and mortuary science. It lists scholarship information and study programs by state. http://www.abfse.org

The **Funeral Service Foundation** is a charitable organization whose purpose is to provide resources for career and professional development; public awareness and education; and the improvement of children's lives. It has played an active role in promoting the role of women in the funeral service industry. It awards scholarships to promising students in mortuary science. http://www.funeralservicefoundation.org

Retirement Home Manager

Retirement Home Manager

Career Compasses

Managing a retirement home takes an array of diverse traits and abilities.

Organizational Skills to manage priorities, workflow, and details (25%)

Communication Skills to be in close touch with residents and fellow managers (25%)

Caring for the elderly who have entrusted their well-being to you (40%)

Ability to Manage Stress when client problems and conflicting priorities intrude (10%)

Destination: Retirement Home Manager

The job of being a retirement home manager can be as varied as the kinds of retirement homes available to manage. A retirement community can be like a vacation resort for those in relative good health. It can also be an elaborate complex that provides a continuum of care for everyone, from those who live independently to those who need skilled nursing care 24/7. Some retirement communities are single-facility homes, while others are part of nationwide chains. Both types can operate either as for-profit or nonprofit corporations.

The various facility types provide the range of choices for seniors: independent living facilities offer housing, meals, housekeeping services, transportation, security, and special amenities like indoor pools and other services; assisted living facilities provide most of the above for those who are unable to live independently but who do not need nursing care; nursing centers provide 24-hour nursing care, rehabilitation services, and assistance with daily tasks for those who cannot care for themselves; and continuing care communities include independent and assisted living, plus a nursing care option, on one campus. In addition, there are businesses that provide home and community-based services, such as adult day care for those who live at home but spend most of their day with other seniors in a supervised facility. There are also organizations that provide services to neighborhoods with very high concentrations of senior citizens. For more about these "naturally occurring retirement communities," go to http://www.norc.com.

Essential Gear

American Association of Homes and Services for the Aging. The Web site of this organization describes the activities of its 5,700-member nonprofit providers that offer a variety of services and facilities for the elderly, including adult day services, home health care, housing, assisted living residences, continuing care retirement communities, and nursing homes.   http://www.aahsa .org

Anyone who wants to go into any aspect of retirement community management should have a special interest in the lives and well being of older people. Your understanding of the needs of seniors and your ability to bring warmth and good humor to the people you serve will carry you far in this occupation. Remember that your clients have survived many challenges over a long journey, but they are now approaching the homestretch of their lives. They deserve all the support they can get.

It also helps greatly to be a multitasker. Even in the most defined of jobs you are likely to face more than one pressing problem simultaneously. Among these problems might be budget shortfalls, food service slipups, medical emergencies involving staff or residents, or scheduling conflicts. Among other business and financial skills, your ability to plan a budget and bring it in reasonably close to estimate will also be highly desirable. The degree of specialization in the role of a retirement home manager depends on the size of the facility. Smaller single-facility homes could have one manager in charge of real estate management, food purchasing, and medical care. Larger facilities may have a different manager for each of those three jobs plus others as well, such as marketing.

Educational requirements for retirement home managers vary according to the type of facility and the state where it is located. You may need as little as one year of college plus six years of experience, or you might require a B.A. or M.A. degree in health facility administration at an accredited institution. Executive directors of all nursing homes and many assisted-living facilities must also have a license issued by the Board of Examiners of Nursing Home Administrators. Community associations that specialize in older people often hire college graduates with little but a degree in business administration of real estate to manage these facilities. Persons with experience working with senior citizens will have an advantage in applying for such positions. Whatever job you aim for in the growing retirement home industry, you will find your talents welcome. While seniors can be demanding in their needs and desires, they can also be very appreciative of the services you provide.

You Are Here

Your journey to a career as a retirement home manager begins with a real fondness and respect for the elders among us.

Do you enjoy interacting with elderly people? Our elders are the survivors of long lives, and each senior citizen has a unique set of memories. Seniors bring a special insight to life because of their vast experience and perspective. Elders appreciate the warmth and interest you show in them. They also enjoy getting the different point of view of a person who is very likely to be much younger than they are.

Are you good at encouraging teamwork? As a leader in the retirement community, retirement home managers take pride in setting an example not only for residents but also for other employees. Managers interact comfortably with everyone from the room cleaners to department heads, and they encourage cooperation.

Navigating the Terrain

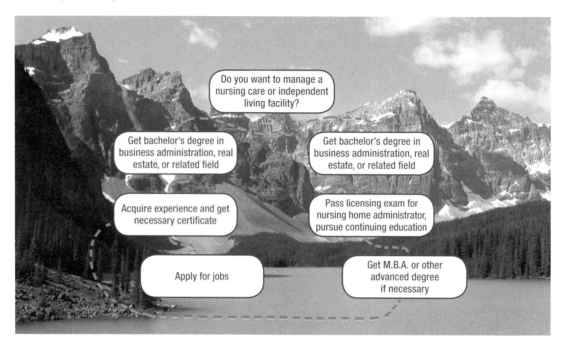

Do you want to manage a nursing care or independent living facility?

Get bachelor's degree in business administration, real estate, or related field

Get bachelor's degree in business administration, real estate, or related field

Acquire experience and get necessary certificate

Pass licensing exam for nursing home administrator, pursue continuing education

Apply for jobs

Get M.B.A. or other advanced degree if necessary

Do your strengths also include organizational, business, and financial skills? Retirement home managers need experience in these areas, especially in smaller establishments where they usually wear several hats. For example, they may oversee not only the budget, but also marketing efforts and personnel, and they need to know how to prioritize their tasks.

Organizing Your Expedition

Before you set out, know where you are going.

Decide on a destination. As we have seen, there are many types of retirement facilities for seniors, but working effectively in all of them depends on your basic understanding, respect, and love of elderly people. By volunteering at a local retirement home, you can test your interest and commitment to this kind of work by talking with residents, sharing their activities, and helping them with chores when necessary. If you are now working in related field, such as community recreation, food service, or nursing, you may even be able to obtain paid work in a retirement home as an independent or outside contractor. Use this opportunity to get to know individuals in different areas within the retirement community, whether it be in marketing, personal services, or finances. Ask these individuals about their jobs. You may discover a niche that feels especially right for you.

Scout the terrain. Take the opportunity to investigate the different types of senior living arrangements—independent or assisted living facilities, nursing centers, or continuing care communities—to see how they differ and which environment seems most comfortable to you as a potential place of employment. The atmosphere at a nursing home is obviously going to be quite different from that in an independent living facility. You may feel more comfortable working with seniors who, like yourself, are still active and mobile. Yet many find meaning and satisfaction in helping those who are less able to take care of themselves. If you have no special preference, then working in a continuing care community where there are all types of seniors could be your most attractive option.

Go back to school. While some retirement homes may require a minimum of education beyond a bachelor's degree, many—especially those that administer health care—may require an M.S. or other advanced degree and eligibility for licensing as a nursing home administrator (NHA). Because of past scandals in which unscrupulous administrators abused or neglected vulnerable seniors, government heavily regulates the nursing home industry. In New York State, for example, applicants to be a nursing home administrator must:

a) be 21 years of age or older;
b) satisfactorily answer questions about their "character and suitability" within a prescribed time period:
c) complete a four-year or master's degree in a related field such as health care administration; OR three or more years of recent qualifying field experience; OR two or more years as an administrator of an out-of-state nursing facility;
d) successfully complete a 12–24 month training program or have equivalent field experience to qualify for licensing;

Notes from the Field
David Urso
Manager of marketing and resident services
Hanover, New Hampshire

What were you doing before you decided to change careers?

I had been managing the food service operations at Kendal-Hanover, a life-care retirement community in New Hampshire, as part of a large outside company that had a food service contract with Kendal. I worked in the dining services department for over six years before the opportunity to move to Marketing presented itself.

Why did you change your career?

First and foremost is the satisfaction that is derived from working with seniors. I find this population to be very genuine, honest, and appreciative. In the corporate dining area where I had previously worked, the question was "How am I going to get another quarter out of that person's pocket when they come for lunch?" In the nonprofit world the goal is to work within budget and make sure the diner is happy. I also left food service because I wanted new challenges and I did not want to relocate.

How did you make the transition?

I recognized that in order for me to create opportunities for myself, I was going to have to further my education. I started an MBA in

e) complete 15 credits of required course work above the beginning level in nursing home administration, health care financial management, and legal issues in health care;

f) pass a written licensing test.

Landmarks

If you are in your twenties . . . Young people often receive a special welcome in a retirement community, since this age group is relatively scarce among a disproportionately elderly population. This situation can make your job hunt a relatively easy one at the entry level.

Leadership program at a local university. Fortunately, the contracting company was paying my tuition. During the enrollment process, I asked my immediate supervisor, the CFO, and the CEO to write letters of recommendation for me. This signaled them that I was serious about my career and moving upward within the organization. When Kendal saw how successfully I was managing the dining program while also attending school, their CEO asked to meet with me and discuss my career goals. He advised me to take some risks and not put myself in a box as just a food service manager. Several weeks later, I asked my supervisor if I could be considered for the director of marketing position that had been vacant for almost a year. I told him I enjoyed working with the residents but was looking for new challenges. After several discussions with our Executive Director, the organization was restructured to create my new position.

What are the keys to success in your career?

As director of Marketing and Resident Services I think it is crucial to have a clear understanding of your organization and what it is you are marketing. It is easy to say that I am marketing a retirement community, but it is important to know what makes us different from other retirement communities. Having been at Kendal for over six years, it was easy for me to move to marketing because I knew the community.

If you are in your thirties or forties . . . If you have experience working with elders, especially in a related area like food service, community recreation, or financial management, your skills can fill a needed gap in many retirement communities. Consider taking courses in these areas that can make you stand out among other applicants.

If you are in your fifties . . . Especially if your financial situation permits, or if your current employer is able to support your continuing education, you should consider getting an advanced degree in business or other related field that will make you a more attractive candidate for administrative positions.

If you are over sixty . . . At this stage in life, your age can be a definite asset, since you are more likely to understand and be able to relate to the concerns of residents in a retirement community. Take advantage of this asset by putting together a résumé that emphasizes your experiences with the elderly.

Essential Gear

My Mother Your Mother: Embracing "Slow Medicine," the Compassionate Approach to Caring for Your Aging Loved Ones **(HarperCollins, 2008).** Dennis McCullough, M.D., presents an empathic philosophy for caring for those over the age of 80 in this book. The author defines eight stations of late life, shows how to assess an elderly person's condition, emphasizes the need for caregivers to have a support team, shows how to navigate the medical bureaucracy, and describes how the process of dying can bring elders and their families closer.

Further Resources

The **National Council on Aging** is a nonprofit service and advocacy organization for older adults, especially the disadvantaged and vulnerable, and the community organizations that serve them. The NCOA's goal is to improve the lives of older Americans by creating and leading multi-sector partnerships and alliances and organizing nationwide networks of organizations and leaders.   http://www.ncoa.org

The **Assisted Living Federation of America** is the largest national association devoted to professionally operated assisted living facilities for seniors. Their web site's comprehensive career center enables users to post their résumés and view jobs available nationwide.   http://alfa.org

Personal Assistant

Personal Assistant

Career Compasses

Take stock of the main skills a personal assistant needs.

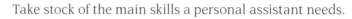

Relevant knowledge that will expand the services you can offer (20%)

Organizational Skills to keep track of the many and changing demands of clients (20%)

Communication Skills to keep attuned to the needs of many kinds of people (20%)

Caring about making clients feel productive and satisfied (40%)

Destination: Personal Assistant

Personal assistants go by many names: concierge, lifestyle manager, virtual assistant, errand runner. Whether buying theater or concert tickets for hotel guests, arranging corporate meetings, or handling a private client's correspondence, concierges share a common goal: to provide useful services that save their clients valuable time. As a personal assistant or concierge (the two most common occupation titles) you may work for a hotel, apartment building, corporation, or concierge company. You may also form your own company to offer concierge services.

Concierge is a French word that in medieval times referred to a high official in the palaces and castles of the nobility. The concierge kept the keys to every room in the estate and lighted the visitor's way with candles. (*Concierge* comes from the phrase *Comte des Cierges*—literally "keeper of the candles.") We see the original meaning of the word today when a mayor presents a visiting celebrity the "keys to the city." Instead of literal keys, concierges today offer services that their clients are too busy or unable to carry out themselves. These services may vary depending on whether the concierge works for a hotel, a corporation, or individual clients. In a hotel, your clients are transients whom you may never meet again. Corporate concierges, on the other hand, may handle the business affairs of a single executive or be in charge of coordinating group events like business meetings and corporate dinners. Concierges with individual clients are usually called personal assistants. They function like executive secretaries to their employers.

Essential Gear

Ultimate Service: The Complete Handbook to the World of the Concierge (Prentice Hall, 1994). This volume by Holly Stiel is designed as a textbook for courses in hotel management and service. It covers such topics as building relationships, telephone manners, and handling difficult clients.

If you enjoy serving the material or professional needs of others, then being a concierge can be a satisfying career. Becoming a concierge does not require a college degree—at least not at first. If you do at some point feel the need for more education, a college degree in business, marketing, or hotel and hospitality management will stand you in good stead. More basic requirements for a beginning concierge are an innate sense of organization, an ability to communicate with all kinds of people, an enthusiasm for the job, and—above all—the desire to please others. Concierges who want to advance will have the kind of curiosity and drive that are the marks of the true entrepreneur—the desire to learn everything one can about a particular business in order to find areas in which they can offer new services. Many successful concierges have turned a special passion—for example, fashion, entertainment, art and antiques, or any of dozens of other areas—into a marketable service.

Two relatively recent developments in today's population have increased the need for concierge services. One is the growing number of wealthy people who are accustomed to having others cater to their needs. For example, managers of expensive hotels have found that having a concierge service increases their attractiveness to guests. Expanding on this attraction, concierges today have also found growing niches in gated residential communities, high-end office buildings, and exclusive retail stores.

Another cause of the increased demand for concierges is the swelling number of elderly, particularly hospital patients. This increase in the number of senior citizens has led to the emergence of the medical concierge, who functions like a hotel concierge but within a hospital or clinic. Working especially with out-of-town patients, the medical concierge may assist them in coordinating multiple doctor appointments and making them feel as comfortable as possible. The medical concierge also helps the patient's visiting relatives by providing information about leisure activities, making hotel and airline reservations, and arranging taxi and car service pickups. Many hospitals also offer medical concierge services to their own employees as well. These workers, from doctors to support staff, often work long shifts and appreciate this service just as much as patients do.

Essential Gear

***The Concierge Manual,* 3rd edition (New Road Publishing, 2007).** Katherine C. and Ron Giovanni's book is a comprehensive look at different forms of concierge service, ranging from small boutiques to large corporations. Topics covered include business plans, Web site development, fee structure, vendor services, and sales and marketing.

Becoming a concierge is a process in which doors to growth and new opportunities can open at any time. Your "open sesame" to a new career may begin with something as simple as a well-worded ad on a strategically selected bulletin board, or a well-placed call to a contact with little free time and a large disposable income. Or you may start out by applying to a large corporation or hotel that maintains a staff of concierges. The concierge profession is growing fast and spilling out into new areas like medicine and the law, so a Web search may find new organizations seeking to capitalize on this popularity. For the person with the ambition and the desire to explore fresh fields, concierge may be an ideal vehicle for a new career.

You Are Here

The length of your path to becoming a concierge depends partly on how well you can assess and develop your strengths and interests concerning the job.

Do you enjoy helping other people lead more efficient, successful, and happier lives? As a hotel concierge you may be asked to save your hotel guests time by ordering their theater tickets and making their dinner reservations. As a corporate concierge you may plan corporate parties, dinners, and other events. As a personal assistant you could be shopping for clients' gifts, taking care of their emails and correspondence, or paying their bills. Your roles will vary depending on whom you work for and your own areas of expertise.

Do people compliment you on your sense of organization and ability to communicate? Important aspects of being a concierge include

Navigating the Terrain

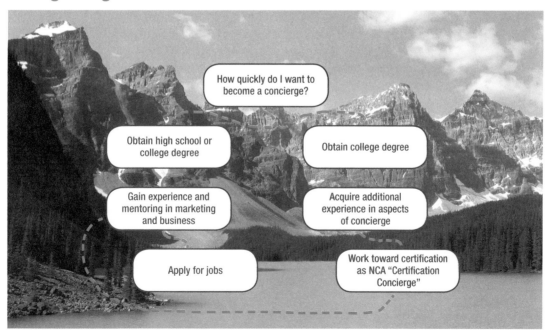

How quickly do I want to become a concierge?

Obtain high school or college degree

Obtain college degree

Gain experience and mentoring in marketing and business

Acquire additional experience in aspects of concierge

Apply for jobs

Work toward certification as NCA "Certification Concierge"

Notes from the Field
Sheryl Novak
Concierge
Chicago, Illinois

What were you doing before you decided to change careers?

I got married right out of high school and had two children over the next decade. I was working part time driving a bus and being a supervisor for a park district after-school program, bringing my children along with me.

Why did you change your career?

I realized that my marriage was not going to last. I looked into a "displaced homemaker" program at a local college. I thought I had better go to college and get a degree, as I was going to be a single mother. While attending a speech class, we took turns telling the class what we did for a living, and a young lady explained her job as a concierge. I realized that I had all the talents needed for that job!

How did you make the transition?

With a mortgage to pay and a family to feed, I realized I could not afford to go back to college. So I went to the very hotel that the young lady worked for (I had no idea there were other choices!) and put in an application. After meeting with several of the managers, I was hired! I

being able to understand and keep track of multiple requests from your clients, prioritize your tasks, and plan your day to make the best use of your time. As you juggle multiple tasks, you need to be able to stay focused on the task at hand while not forgetting what remains to be done.

Do you have an entrepreneurial spirit? The best concierges are always looking for ways to expand their skills and range of services to meet changing demands. While a college degree is not necessary for most entry-level jobs in this field, concierges who advance to higher levels are more likely to have a college degree in subjects like business or marketing.

worked hard every day at the job and was willing to learn any new job within the hotel when asked. I read every hospitality brochure and book on concierge services I could find and took every class offered by the hotel on customer service, problem solving, etc. Later I also worked as a corporate concierge before opening my own concierge business.

What are the keys to success in your career?

One—jump in! I have been scared to death at each turn in my career, but pushed on anyway. I asked questions, worked hard, and watched people who were successful in their chosen careers. I joined an association that supports the concierge and hospitality community and said yes to opportunities to lead and give back.

Two—dare to dream! I mapped out my company while I was still a hotel concierge. Working for someone else gave me the tools and knowledge to create my own company and make it better.

Three—listen to the little voice! Believe in yourself. I am the only one in my family to own, create, and run a business—and I did it as a single parent! Don't let other peoples' doubts and fears be projected onto you.

Four—one step at a time! Everything I did yesterday takes me to the place I am today—from hotel concierge to corporate concierge to business owner—one step at a time, sometimes baby steps—but always forward! When you're tired after an unproductive day, count your blessings and past successes, get some rest, and begin again!

Organizing Your Expedition

Before you set out, know where you are going.

Decide on a destination. Do you want to work for yourself or for someone else? Do you want to work in a hotel, the headquarters of a corporation, or in the office of a busy executive or celebrity? The concierge's potential domain is so large that you may not end up where you thought you would, but it helps to aim for a specific niche since your choice will partly determine the kind of skills you need to hone. Hotel guests are transients with predictable requests: sightseeing and dining suggestions, directions to local landmarks, and the like. Corporations may have visiting bigwigs with similar requests, but you will also assist in planning corporate events. Busy executives and celebrities may be the most unpredictable clients to assist—at least until you get to know them. Decide which clientele you would feel most comfortable in serving.

Scout the terrain. Research the companies and individuals in the domain you have chosen. Design your résumé to emphasize the skills and experience you feel are most pertinent to that domain. Join the local chapter of the National Concierge Association and use their Web site to make contacts in the field. Use any personal contacts you may have to seek informational interviews that may get your foot in the door and eventually lead to a job. In the process of doing all these things you will learn a lot not only about being a concierge but also about what you have to offer the profession.

Find the path that's right for you. Through your research, interviews, and networking you should get a much clearer idea of the best matches between your skills and the possible niches into which you might best fit. If your office skills—knowledge of computer applications, filing systems, record keeping, and so on—are especially strong, you may find that the corporate or executive concierge path is your best bet. Do not rule out other niches, however, where you may need the same skills. Know your strengths, but keep your options flexible. You may not end up where you thought you would, but that is part of the adventure in entering the expanding, changing world of the concierge.

Landmarks

If you are in your twenties . . . If you were the child in your family who always could be counted on to help when asked, you may have a natural talent for this profession. Assess your strengths and offer your services in a carefully worded ad that you can post locally or online. Investigate local establishments that offer concierge services, or find one by using such sites as http://www.errandinfo.com. Talk to concierges and develop a network of contacts that can help you get started.

If you are in your thirties or forties . . . If you have developed transferable skills through other service jobs, translate them into concierge qualifications on a résumé. Pursue networking opportunities afforded on such Web sites as http://www.cieaweb.org, which lists names, email and snail-mail addresses, and telephone numbers for almost all 636 of its members in the United States, Canada, and throughout the English-speaking world.

If you are in your fifties . . . With some transferable experience under your belt, try asking those you have helped to provide you with written testimonials to your skills in assisting people. A quotable business reference can go a long way in verifying your experience in this field.

If you are over sixty . . . If you have energy to keep up with what can be a fast pace in this occupation, there are plenty of clients who will prefer the discretion, wisdom, and perspective of an older person when considering to whom to entrust their personal or business affairs.

Further Resources

As stated on its Web site, the **National Concierge Association's** founding principle is "to provide unlimited and unparalleled networking and educational opportunities to its members . . . as well as to promote the industry worldwide." http://www.nationalconciergeassociation.com
The **American Errand Runners Organization (AERO)** lists as its goals as: promoting the industry, educating the public, assisting those who want to start their own errand running business, publishing information on industry trends and new practices, and establishing a centralized list of errand services. http://www.errandinfo.com

Professional Organizer

Professional Organizer

Career Compasses

Organizing is a profession in which four skill sets may be equally important.

Relevant Knowledge of the niche in which you are operating, whether it is someone's closets, a deceased's estate, or a major business (25%)

Organizational Skills that are useful in your particular niche (25%)

Communication Skills to translate concepts and methods of organization into action plans (25%)

Caring about the people whom you are helping to get organized (25%)

Destination: Professional Organizer

The average American spends almost an hour a day looking for things they own but cannot find, according to a 2004 poll quoted in *Newsweek*. Eighty percent of what we keep we never use, says the *Agency Sales Magazine*. These statistics suggest an epidemic of disorganization that affects the ability of many people to lead fully productive lives. Challenging this massive clutter are the members of a new and currently hot occupation: professional organizer. Less than 30 years ago, a national association for this kind of job did not exist. Today the growing National Association of Professional Organizers boasts 4,300 members throughout the United States and eight foreign countries.

Professional organizers must possess basic skills in space planning, time management, and general organization. One of the attractions of this occupation, however, is the number of different niches that exist within the job for those who wish to specialize. Professional organizers who are just starting out may find themselves doing something as seemingly mundane as organizing closets or planning office spaces. Do enough of that kind of work, however, and you may find yourself in demand as a specialist in those areas. Other areas of expertise include—but certainly are not limited to—relocation

Essential Gear

It's All Too Much (**Free Press, 2007**). This informative book by Peter Walsh focuses in on how to get rid of the material "stuff" in your life that is keeping you from being the person you want to be. Walsh encourages his readers to ask themselves honestly if each item crammed in their attics or closets is really helping them lead the kind of life they want to lead. If the answer is no, says Walsh, then that item needs to go.

assistance, estate sales, financial organization, health care for seniors, computers as organizing tools, or seminars and workshops on organizing. In short, professional organizing is an occupation whose possibilities for variety and growth are limited only by the range of your own skills and experience. For example, if your specialty involves spatial organization, you need to be able to visualize how you want your space to look. In all areas, you will also need communication skills and flexibility in your thinking so that your solutions meet the client's needs, not yours.

As you have probably suspected, the several possible career paths to becoming a professional organizer reflect the variety of skill sets one can bring to the job. It is possible to enter the field with as little as an A.A. degree and some business experience, but most will want to pursue a four-year degree or more, depending on your resources and other responsibilities. In any case, experience in a business environment is extremely valuable. Most professional organizers run their operations as small businesses, so you will need bookkeeping and marketing as well as organizing skills. If your business is a start-up, it may take time to build up a clientele, so you will probably need savings or a credit line to draw on at the beginning. Taking on a partner will help you share the financial burden. Many also find that working with another person is much more productive than working alone, especially if both partners have complementary skills.

Let's assume your business is established and you have documented 1,500 hours of professional organizing experience, of which up to 250 hours may consist of college degrees and continuing education or other experience such as teleclasses, conferences, and similar activities. You may now wish to seek designation as a Certified Professional Organizer (CPO) as developed by the National Association of Professional Organizers. The Web site http://www.certifiedprofessionalorganizers.org describes requirements for becoming a CPO. In addition to the 1,500-hour stipulation, requirements include passing a two-hour computer-based examination on a properly conducted job task analysis, as well as passing a two-hour pencil-and-paper test covering the four main aspects of the job. These are: making a preliminary assessment, developing and implementing an action plan, evaluating the results, and being familiar with legal and ethical issues in the profession. To maintain their CPO designation, professional organizers must be recertified every three years by either (a) affirming 1,000 hours of paid work in an area relating to organizing, plus 45 hours of continuing education related to organizing during the preceding three-year period; or (b) retaking the examination.

Essential Gear

***It's Hard to Make a Difference When You Can't Find Your Keys* (Penguin, 2004).** Marilyn Paul's study of disorganization tackles the problem from both a psychological and a philosophical point of view. Paul lays out a kind of spiritual path that begins with finding one's real purpose in becoming organized. For Paul, that purpose is not neatness for neatness's sake, but rather to see ourselves in relation to others and to the world around us.

With or without the CPO designation, professional organizing can be a rewarding career. You are helping people make their lives more productive. At the end of a project you will also have visible proof of your success in a tidier set of closets, a streamlined computer or hard-copy filing system, or a happily relocated business or family. You can expect similar results in any number of areas in which professional organizers find their niches.

You Are Here

Your journey to becoming a professional organizer can begin from many different places.

Do you find pleasure in bringing a sense of order to places, things, and events? Professional organizers usually help their clients first develop a clear vision of their goals in life. Then they help clients strive daily to make changes that will bring them closer to realizing these goals. For example, professional organizers know how to help people put things in their proper places, arrive at their appointments on time, and prioritize their activities so the important things get done first. They also encourage clients to take time to reflect on their goals and the actions necessary to achieve them.

Do you like to help friends with organization problems improve their lives? Do you find that others come to you for advice on work problems and later thank you for helping them? Then you probably have the ability to listen and infer what the other person means. You will also need to be a good teacher who can ask the kinds of questions that will inspire clients to find answers that they can apply to their own lives.

Do you have the mental and physical endurance to stick with a project? Unless they have the funds to hire help, most professional organizers are one-person shops who do everything from helping clients plan a business move to labeling and hauling heavy boxes when moving day comes.

Organizing Your Expedition

Before you set out, know where you are going.

Decide on a destination. Given your natural bent toward organizing, it is equally important to consider the environment in which you want to work. The three main choices are: as an employee of a large company that does organizing, as a partner in a two- or three-person business, or as a one-person operation. This is obviously not an irrevocable decision, but considering your options may help you better define your ultimate goals in

Navigating the Terrain

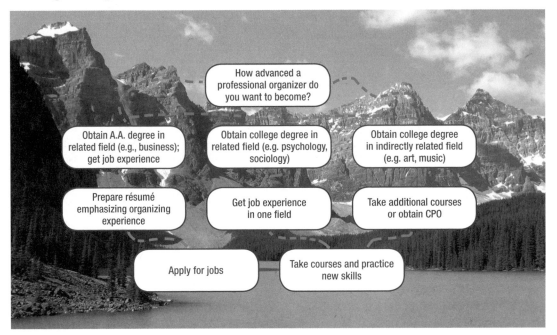

How advanced a professional organizer do you want to become?

Obtain A.A. degree in related field (e.g., business); get job experience

Obtain college degree in related field (e.g. psychology, sociology)

Obtain college degree in indirectly related field (e.g. art, music)

Prepare résumé emphasizing organizing experience

Get job experience in one field

Take additional courses or obtain CPO

Apply for jobs

Take courses and practice new skills

seeking this career. Do not forget to think about how your previous education and work history can segue into a career in professional organizing.

Scout the terrain. Do not rule out any particular field when you are just starting out. Which will be your eventual cash cow: closets or kitchens? Estates? Relocation assistance? Financial records? Health care bill tracking? Computers as organizing tools? Some combination of the above? Do some research, see which areas attract you, and pursue the most interesting ones. You should also consider how much additional education you are willing and able to devote to your career—A.A. degree; B.A.; or advanced degree(s)—since this may affect the number of organizing niches you are qualified to pursue down the road.

Find the path that's right for you. When seeking organizing jobs sat the beginning of your career, you may have to work for very little to gain experience, but that will pay off later in at least two ways. First, you will have a better idea of your strengths and interests. Second, you will have

Notes from the Field

Angela Wallace
Professional organizer
Novato, California

What were you doing before you decided to change careers?

After majoring in geography in college, living abroad for 4 years, and getting an M.A. in international administration, I held a job that involved project management and union negotiations. I had previously been temporary manager of a store. With that background, I bought and operated a gourmet coffee and candy shop for 3 ½ years. It was a place where people liked to stop and chat and bring their problems, and I found that I really enjoyed socializing and giving advice to folks.

Why did you change your career?

I lost the lease on my store. After thinking about it, I decided that I'd been giving out free information for years and it was time to start charging. I helped people move, gave advice on business problems, and they found that just talking with me helped them organize their thoughts. I found that I was very good at it.

something to show to potential clients who require experience. By following this process, and pursuing your continuing education through in-person or online courses, seminars, workshops, conferences, and networking with other organizers, you will eventually find the path that is right for you. A degree or certificate in computer science, for example, could lead you to a career helping people use computers to organize their filing systems and records.

Landmarks

If you are in your twenties . . . As a self-proclaimed "neatnik," you may be able to parlay your talent into a new career simply by offering to bring a similar order to your friends' possessions, collections, memorabilia, and

How did you make the transition?

When I started out in this business, nobody knew what a professional organizer was. When you said you were an organizer, people assumed you meant union organizer. At first I did almost any job that came along. For a while I was housecleaning, or I worked with elderly to organize their health care. I covered retail stores as a sales assistant when the owner was gone. Once I ran a retail store set up to honor the U.N.'s 50th anniversary. My advice to budding professional organizers is to take whatever comes your way, until you find out what you really like.

What are the keys to success in your career?

Organizing is a broad occupation with many niches. I have no interest in organizing people's closets, garages, or estates. My niche is business organization. After 23 years as a professional organizer, I've found that perseverance, creativity, passion, courage, and problem-solving and computer skills are all important in my work. I help business owners plan the changes they need to make in order to succeed. For example, do they need to hire more people or fire them? My advice is to get educated on anything and everything that you think will help you to succeed. For example, right now I'm in a year-long sales training program.

other such things. Community bulletin board or online listings, word of mouth, or other advertising of your skill in extreme makeovers will give you a foot in the door of paid professional organizing positions.

If you are in your thirties or forties . . . Having acquired valuable experience in organizing your own life, it is probably time to get some educational validation of your skills through courses, workshops, and seminars. This is not only a valuable way to gain useful knowledge in the field, but also a good way to make contacts with potential future partners or mentors.

If you are in your fifties . . . Look at your interests, strengths, previous experience, and education, and make connections to particular niches in the professional organizing business. Your special interest and knowledge of memorabilia, records management, business relocation, or many other subgroups will give you a leg up on younger people without first-hand experience in these areas.

If you are over sixty . . . Again, as an older person you are now in a position to be an expert in areas such as health care that may be only theoretical possibilities to those in their twenties and thirties. If you have the energy and drive to take advantage of your first-hand experience in a particular niche, you can make a successful transition to professional organizing.

Further Resources

National Organization of Professional Organizers (NAPO) is the only organization that offers, through its chapters, a training course leading to designation as a CPO—Certified Professional Organizer. Its Web site an invaluable source of information about how to get started in this business. http://www.napo.net

The purpose of the **National Study Group on Chronic Disorganization (NSGCD)** is to benefit those affected by this condition through exploring, developing, and communicating "information, organizing techniques, and solutions to professional organizers, related professionals, and the public," according their Web site. http://www.nsgcd.org

Event Planner

Event Planner

Compass Points

Keep your eye on the skill areas that you will need to juggle as an event planner.

Caring about the needs and desires of your clients (25%)

Communication Skills in determining what is required for an event to succeed (25%)

Organizational Skills to coordinate the many aspects of a complex happening (40%)

Mathematical Skills to measure, for example, numbers of people, amounts of food, and necessary space (10%)

Destination: Event Planner

Do you like to throw parties and bring people together to have fun, share information about common interests, or for any number of other purposes? Then you may be a candidate for professional event planner. Do you also thrive when sweating the details involved in bringing off such events—meeting tight schedules, lugging display materials, thinking quickly to solve last-minute problems? Then you could be a *serious* candidate in this field where jobs are expected to increase 20 percent, or faster than average, over the next six or seven years.

Event planners often coordinate each aspect of organizing a meeting or a convention. They must translate the theme of the event into specific terms by helping to choose speakers, hire entertainment, and arrange for printed materials and AV equipment, among many other things. They are involved in recommending or selecting the site for the event, as well as choosing the various suppliers of lodging, food and beverages, transportation, telecommunications, and other required goods or services. Planners negotiate the terms of contracts with these suppliers and are responsible for providing a detailed budget that estimates the cost of every aspect of the event. During the meeting or convention, they are busy registering attendees and carrying out the plans made earlier regarding food, beverages, lodging, and transportation. After the event is over, they analyze questionnaire responses to measure how well the meeting or convention achieved its purpose.

Essential Gear

The Business of Event Planning (Wiley, 2002). Author Judy Allen describes all the major steps in planning and producing a successful special event, including preparing proposals, negotiating and writing up contracts, setting fees, using new technologies, and attending to safety issues.

Event planners may work for themselves or for various for-profit or nonprofit companies of varying sizes. If the event is too large and complex for a one-person shop to handle, the sponsoring organization will turn to an event planning company. Here one planner may handle the financial planning and contracts, another planner the program arrangements, a third the telecommunications set-up, and so on. The job outlook for event planners can vary considerably depending on the sector in which you work. The demand for corporate planners varies according to the business cycle. Nonprofit associations may offer steadier employment since, unlike corporate conventions, associations design their conventions to produce revenue. During an economic recession, however, the only organizations that maintain their meeting and convention planning staffs are those that require attendance in order to maintain their members' licenses, such as the health care industry.

A bachelor's degree was recently held by only about half of all event planners, since much of what you learn is on the job. As meetings and conventions become more complex, however, a college degree is more likely to be a requirement. Much of the training will continue to be on the job. Events planners often start out by learning one task like reviewing contracts or planning small meetings before advancing to larger jobs. As they gain experience in a specific aspect of event planning—say, meeting planning—many event planners seek the Certified Meeting Professional (CMP) credential offered by the Convention Industry Council as an aid in career advancement. Those who qualify must have at least three years of meeting planning experience, a full-time job in meeting management, and proof of successfully completed meetings. A similar certification in special events, the Certified Special Events Professional (CSEP) designation is offered by the International Special Events Society. Upon successful completion of an application and a suggested ten years in the industry, Global Certification in Meeting Management (CMM) can result from an intensive, 5-day residential program administered by Meeting Professionals International.

Event planners need a variety of skills to be successful, including written and verbal communication skills and the ability to relate to individuals from many backgrounds and cultures. Conventions are increasingly international in scope, and the ability to speak several languages is a big advantage. Event planners must also bring quantitative, analytical, and computer skills to bear as they make estimates and draw up budgets. Since the body of knowledge required from meeting to meeting can vary considerably, event planners must also have the curiosity and drive to read up on each new industry they encounter so that they intelligently plan programs that deal with the key issues facing each industry.

You Are Here

Your path to becoming an event planner begins with a strong desire to bring people together to share information and enjoy good times.

Do you love to plan events that make those who attend feel happy and fulfilled? If you feel that the desire to party, as well as to meet for serious business-related purposes, is a basic human need, then you may be an ideal candidate to become an event planner. You will need communication and organizational skills to bring together the key players in these events and determine how you can best meet their goals.

Do you enjoy coordinating multiple activities within a fixed time period? You will need to be a multitasker to thrive in this field. Event planners may manage anything and everything from the space requirements for an event to the food needs of the event attendees. Did we mention planning and meeting a budget, negotiating contracts with suppliers, and arranging support services, just to name a few other tasks?

Are you willing to work irregular hours doing unglamorous chores in order to make an event a success? An event planner is not always meeting interesting people, taste-testing gourmet delicacies, or choosing expensive floral displays. Event planners also do tedious jobs like carrying heavy boxes of convention materials, sweating tight deadlines, and working late for days on end.

Navigating the Terrain

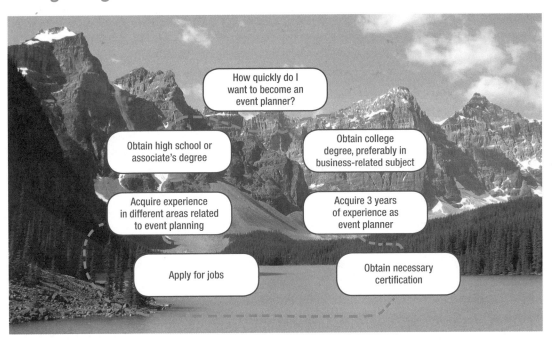

Notes from the Field

Cindy Y. Lo
Event planner
Austin, Texas

What were you doing before you decided to change careers?

I was an assistant project manager and technical consultant for a local software company that sold custom software solutions. While in college I had been an intern two consecutive summers for Procter & Gamble, doing sales and business management.

Why did you change your career?

I was traveling too much, and I really wanted to stay and get to know the city where I lived. I honestly didn't know what I was going to do. When one of my friends suggested event planning, since I was always volunteering for nonprofits while I worked full time for the software company, I [thought], "Hmm . . . I guess I can do this for a living." First, I did try to find someone to work for, but no one was hiring, unfortunately. I had majored in business at college, so I put together a business plan (after interviewing a few other meeting planners and suppliers in

Organizing Your Expedition

Before you set out, know where you are going.

Decide on a destination. Your interest in organizing events can be broad enough to include everything from private parties to national conventions, or specialized enough to focus only on weddings or government gatherings. You may work for firms as varied as convention and trade show organizing firms and associated industries (39 percent of all meeting planning jobs); nonprofit, charitable, or professional organizations (27 percent); hotels (17 percent); educational services (8 percent); sole proprietorships—that is, yourself (6 percent); and local, state or national governments (3 percent). Talk to event planners in different kinds of organizations and decide which feel more comfortable to you. If none of these leaps out at you, however, do not worry. Many event planners the industry) and started *Red Velvet Events.* Since my dad is a business owner himself, I already knew first-hand what time commitment it meant. I figured I would give it a try, however, and if it didn't work out, my friend would stop bugging me, and I could go back to the hi-tech industry.

How did you make the transition?

After developing my business plan, I immediately joined both Meeting Professionals International and the International Special Events Society to educate myself about the industry and to network with others in the industry. I jumped in with both feet and have never really stopped.

What are the keys to success in your career?

I have a true love for this type of work, and I am always eager to learn more about the industry every day. I really don't mind waking up in the morning to work and teach myself new processes and new design. If you ever think that you are "done" learning, then you are going to fail in this field. This industry is extremely fast-paced and customer-service oriented, and if you are not willing to give the best customer service, you can forget about excelling as an event planner.

gradually gain experience in different aspects of the business until they find their niche.

Scout the terrain. Few colleges and universities offer degrees specifically in event planning. College majors in business, marketing, and related subjects will have an advantage. Event planners' natural talents and experience, ability to learn, and can-do outlook are their best calling cards in finding a job. To gain experience, develop contacts by joining professional associations such as the nearest chapter of Meeting Planners International or the International Special Events Society. Use these contacts to seek out job opportunities wherever you can find them. Volunteer to help at events. Do not forget the networking possibilities of LinkedIn or Facebook, especially if you are looking for jobs outside of the area in which you live.

Find the path that's right for you. Again, do not neglect online resources when job hunting. For example, the Professional Convention Management Association provides a career center on its Web site (http://www.pcma.org) where for $25 as a nonmember you can post your résumé, work samples, and personal profiles and search for industry-related positions. PCMA also offers a free e-newsletter called *CareerCenter*.

Landmarks

If you are in your twenties . . . If you are not dependent on paid employment for up to a year, this is the perfect time to pursue unpaid internship and volunteer opportunities that will provide invaluable experience as learn the ropes in this multifaceted industry.

Essential Gear

The Convention Industry Council's *CIC Manual,* 8th edition. This manual is widely regarded as the most comprehensive resource available for managing the basic components of a successful event. It can be ordered online at http://www.mpiweb.org. If you cannot afford the $65.95 nonmember price, try to borrow a copy from a contact in the field to get an idea of what is involved in being an event planner.

If you are in your thirties or forties . . . If you have related education or experience—for example, in food service, the travel or hotel industry, public relations, marketing, or telecommunications, then taking a course in event and meeting management at a local college or university could put you in a good position to segue into a position in the industry.

If you are in your fifties . . . Prove that you have the stamina and enthusiasm to keep up with the younger generation. Your business experience, network of contacts in related industries, and continuing curiosity to learn about new opportunities will be a definite plus when you pursue a career change into event planning.

If you are over sixty . . . Take an inventory of the areas in which you offer a unique perspective—perhaps in health care or senior services. Bolster your knowledge with a short course on event and meeting management. This move could make you an attractive candidate to become an event planner in a particular niche.

Further Resources

Meeting Professionals International maintains a Web site that has information on careers, online education programs, conferences, continuing education, scholarships, and more, much of which is available only to members. There are provisions, however, for discount student memberships. http://www.mpiweb.org

The **International Special Events Society (ISES)** educates and promotes the special events industry through sharing useful business information, fostering cooperation among its members and their chapters, and emphasizing high standards in business practice and professional conduct. ISES developed and administers the CSEP designation. This designation recognizes members' levels of experience, achievements, and ongoing education. http://www.ises.org

Appendix A

Going Solo: Starting Your Own Business

Starting your own business can be very rewarding—not only in terms of potential financial success, but also in the pleasure derived from building something from the ground up, contributing to the community, being your own boss, and feeling reasonably in control of your fate. However, business ownership carries its own obligations—both in terms of long hours of hard work and new financial and legal responsibilities. If you succeed in growing your business, your responsibilities only increase. Many new business owners come in expecting freedom only to find themselves chained tighter to their desks than ever before. Still, many business owners find greater satisfaction in their career paths than do workers employed by others.

The Internet has also changed the playing field for small business owners, making it easier than ever before to strike out on your own. While small mom-and-pop businesses such as hairdressers and grocery stores have always been part of the economic landscape, the Internet has made reaching and marketing to a niche easier and more profitable. This has made possible a boom in *microbusinesses*. Generally, a microbusiness is considered to have under ten employees. A microbusiness is also sometimes called a *SOHO* for "small office/home office."

The following appendix is intended to explain, in general terms, the steps in launching a small business, no matter whether it is selling your Web-design services or opening a pizzeria with business partners. It will also point out some of the things you will need to bear in mind. Remember also that the particular obligations of your municipality, state, province, or country may vary, and that this is by no means a substitute for doing your own legwork. Further suggested reading is listed at the end.

Crafting a Business Plan

It has often been said that success is 1 percent inspiration and 99 percent perspiration. However, the interface between the two can often be hard to achieve. The first step to taking your idea and making it reality is constructing a viable *business plan*. The purpose of a business plan is to think things all the way through, to make sure your ideas really are profitable, and to figure out the "who, what, when, where, why, and how" of your business. It fills in the details for three areas: your goals, why you think they are attainable, and how you plan to get to there. "You need to know where you're going before you take that first step," says Drew Curtis, successful Internet entrepreneur and founder of the popular newsfilter Fark.com.

Take care in writing your business plan. Generally, these documents contain several parts: An *executive summary* stating the essence of the plan; a *market summary* explaining how a need exists for the product and service you will supply and giving an idea of potential profitability by comparing your business to similar organizations; a *company description* which includes your products and services, why you think your organization will succeed, and any special advantages you have, as well as a description of *organization* and *management*; and your *marketing and sales strategy*. This last item should include market highlights and demographic information and trends that relate to your proposal. Also include a *funding request* for the amount of start-up capital you will need. This is supported by a section on *financials*, or the sort of cash flow you can expect, based on market analysis, projection, and comparison with existing companies. Other needed information, such as personal financial history, résumés, legal documents, or pictures of your product, can be placed in *appendices*.

Use your business plan to get an idea of how much startup money is necessary and to discipline your thinking and challenge your preconceived notions before you develop your cash flow. The business plan will tell you how long it will take before you turn a profit, which in turn is linked to how long it will before you will be able to pay back investors or a bank loan—which is something that anyone supplying you with money will want to know. Even if you are planning to subsist on grants or you are not planning on investment or even starting a for-profit company, the discipline imposed by the business plan is still the first step to organizing your venture.

A business plan also gives you a realistic view of your personal financial obligations. How long can you afford to live without regular income? How are you going to afford medical insurance? When will your business begin turning a profit? How much of a profit? Will you need to reinvest your profits in the business, or can you begin living off of them? Proper planning is key to success in any venture.

A final note on business plans: Take into account realistic expected profit minus realistic costs. Many small business owners begin by underestimating start-ups and variable costs (such as electricity bills), and then underpricing their product. This effectively paints them into a corner from which it is hard to make a profit. Allow for realistic market conditions on both the supply and the demand side.

Partnering Up

You should think long and hard about the decision to go into business with a partner (or partners). Whereas other people can bring needed capital, expertise, and labor to a business, they can also be liabilities. The questions you need to ask yourself are:

☞ Will this person be a full and equal partner? In other words, are they able to carry their own weight? Make a full and fair assessment of your potential partner's personality. Going into business with someone who lacks a work ethic, or prefers giving directions to working in the trenches, can be a frustrating experience.

☞ What will they contribute to the business? For instance, a partner may bring in start-up money, facilities, or equipment. However, consider if this is enough of a reason to bring them on board. You may be able to get the same advantages in another way—for instance, renting a garage rather than working out of your partner's. Likewise, doubling skill sets does not always double productivity.

☞ Do they have any liabilities? For instance, if your prospective partner has declared bankruptcy in the past, this can hurt your collective venture's ability to get credit.

☞ Will the profits be able to sustain all the partners? Many start-up ventures do not turn profits immediately, and what little they do produce can be spread thin amongst many partners. Carefully work out the math.

Also bear in mind that going into business together can put a strain on even the best personal relationships. No matter whether it is family, friends, or strangers, keep everything very professional with written agreements regarding these investments. Get everything in writing, and be clear where obligations begin and end. "It's important to go into business with the right people," says Curtis. "If you don't—if it degrades into infighting and petty bickering—it can really go south quickly."

Incorporating. . . or Not

Think long and hard about incorporating. Starting a business often requires a fairly large—and risky—financial investment, which in turn exposes you to personal liability. Furthermore, as your business grows, so does your risk. Incorporating can help you shield yourself from this liability. However, it also has disadvantages.

To begin with, incorporating is not necessary for conducting professional transactions such as obtaining bank accounts and credit. You can do this as a sole proprietor, partnership, or simply by filing a DBA ("doing business as") statement with your local court (also known as "trading as" or an "assumed business name"). The DBA is an accounting entity that facilitates commerce and keeps your business' money separate from your own. However, the DBA does not shield you from responsibility if your business fails. It is entirely possible to ruin your credit, lose your house, and have your other assets seized in the unfortunate event of bankruptcy.

The purpose of incorporating is to shield yourself from personal financial liability. In case the worst happens, only the business' assets can be taken. However, this is not always the best solution. Check your local laws: Many states have laws that prevent a creditor from seizing a non-incorporated small business' assets in case of owner bankruptcy. If you are a corporation, however, the things you use to do business that are owned by the corporation—your office equipment, computers, restaurant refrigerators, and other essential equipment—may be seized by creditors, leaving you no way to work yourself out of debt. This is why it is imperative to consult with a lawyer.

There are other areas in which being a corporation can be an advantage, such as business insurance. Depending on your business needs, insurance can be for a variety of things: malpractice, against delivery failures or spoilage, or liability against defective products or accidents. Furthermore, it is easier to hire employees, obtain credit, and buy health insurance as an organization than as an individual. However, on the downside, corporations are subject to specific and strict laws concerning management and ownership. Again, you should consult with a knowledgeable legal expert.

Among the things you should discuss with your legal expert are the advantages and disadvantages of incorporating in your jurisdiction and which type of incorporation is best for you. The laws on liability and how much of your profit will be taken away in taxes vary widely by state and country. Generally, most small businesses owners opt for *limited liability companies* (LLCs), which gives them more control and a more flexible management structure. (Another possibility is a *limited liability partnership*, or *LLP*, which is especially useful for professionals such as doctors and lawyers.) Finally, there is the *corporation*, which is characterized by transferable ownerships shares, perpetual succession, and, of course, limited liability.

Most small businesses are sole proprietorships, partnerships, or privately-owned corporations. In the past, not many incorporated, since it was necessary to have multiple owners to start a corporation. However, this is changing, since it is now possible in many states for an individual to form a corporation. Note also that the form your business takes is usually not set in stone: A sole proprietorship or partnership can switch to become an LLC as it grows and the risks increase; furthermore, a successful LLC can raise capital by changing its structure to become a corporation and selling stock.

Legal Issues

Many other legal issues besides incorporating (or not) need to be addressed before you start your business. It is impossible to speak directly to every possible business need in this brief appendix, since regulations, licenses, and health and safety codes vary by industry and locality. A restaurant in Manhattan, for instance, has to deal not only with the usual issues such as health inspectors, and the state liquor board, but obscure regulations such as New York City's cabaret laws, which prohibit dancing without a license in a place where alcohol is sold. An asbestos-abatement company, on the other hand, has a very different set of standards it has to abide by, including federal regulations. Researching applicable laws is part of starting up any business.

Part of being a wise business owner is knowing when you need help. There is software available for things like bookkeeping, business plans, and Web site creation, but generally, consulting with a knowledgeable professional—an accountant or a lawyer (or both)—is the smartest move. One of the most common mistakes is believing that just because you have expertise in the technical aspects of a certain field, you know all about running a business in that field. Whereas some people may balk at the expense, by suggesting the best way to deal with possible problems, as well as cutting through red tape and seeing possible pitfalls that you may not even have been aware of, such professionals usually more than make up for their cost. After all, they have far more experience at this than does a first-time business owner!

Financial

Another necessary first step in starting a business is obtaining a bank account. However, having the account is not as important as what you do with it. One of the most common problems with small businesses is undercapitalization—especially in brick-and-mortar businesses that sell or make something, rather than service-based businesses. The rule of thumb is that you should have access to money equal to your first year's anticipated profits, plus start-up expenses. (Note that this is not the same as having the money on hand—see the discussion on lines of credit, below.) For instance, if your annual rent, salaries, and equipment will cost $50,000 and you expect $25,000 worth of profit in your first year, you should have access to $75,000 worth of financing.

You need to decide what sort of financing you will need. Small business loans have both advantages and disadvantages. They can provide critical start-up credit, but in order to obtain one, your personal credit will need to be good, and you will, of course, have to pay them off with interest. In general, the more you and your partners put into the business yourselves, the more credit lenders will be willing to extend to you.

Equity can come from your own personal investment, either in cash or an equity loan on your home. You may also want to consider bringing on partners—at least limited financial partners—as a way to cover start-up costs.

It is also worth considering obtaining a line of credit instead of a loan. A loan is taken out all at once, but with a line of credit, you draw on the money as you need it. This both saves you interest payments and means that you have the money you need when you need it. Taking out too large of a loan can be worse than having no money at all! It just sits there collecting interest—or, worse, is spent on something utterly unnecessary—and then is not around when you need it most.

The first five years are the hardest for any business venture; your venture has about double the usual chance of closing in this time (1 out of 6, rather than 1 out of 12). You will probably have to tighten your belt at home, as well as work long hours and keep careful track of your business expenses. Be careful with your money. Do not take unnecessary risks, play it conservatively, and always keep some capital in reserve for emergencies. The hardest part of a new business, of course, is the learning curve of figuring out what, exactly, you need to do to make a profit, and so the best advice is to have plenty of savings—or a job to provide income—while you learn the ropes.

One thing you should not do is count on venture capitalists or "angel investors," that is, businesspeople who make a living investing on other businesses in the hopes that their equity in the company will increase in value. Venture capitalists have gotten something of a reputation as indiscriminate spendthrifts due to some poor choices made during the dot-com boom of the late 1990s, but the fact is that most do not take risks on unproven products. Rather, they are attracted to young companies that have the potential to become regional or national powerhouses and give better-than-average returns. Nor are venture capitalists endless sources of money; rather, they are savvy businesspeople who are usually attracted to companies that have already experienced a measure of success. Therefore, it is better to rely on your own resources until you have proven your business will work.

Bookkeeping 101

The principles of double-entry bookkeeping have not changed much since its invention in the fifteenth century: one column records debits, and one records credits. The trick is *doing* it. As a small business owner, you need to be disciplined and meticulous at recording your finances. Thankfully, today there is software available that can do everything from tracking payables and receivables to running checks and generating reports.

Honestly ask yourself if you are the sort of person who does a good job keeping track of finances. If you are not, outsource to a bookkeeping company or hire someone to come in once or twice a week to enter invoices and generate checks for you. Also remember that if you have employees or even freelancers, you will have to file tax forms for them at the end of the year.

Another good idea is to have an accountant for your business to handle advice and taxes (federal, state, local, sales tax, etc.). In fact, consulting with a certified public accountant is a good idea in general, since they are usually aware of laws and rules that you have never even heard of.

Finally, keep your personal and business accounting separate. If your business ever gets audited, the first thing the IRS looks for is personal expenses disguised as business expenses. A good accountant can help you to know what are legitimate business expenses. Everything you take from the business account, such as payroll and reimbursement, must be recorded and classified.

Being an Employer

Know your situation regarding employees. To begin with, if you have any employees, you will need an Employer Identification Number (EIN), also sometimes called a Federal Tax Identification Number. Getting an EIN is simple: You can fill out IRS form SS-4, or complete the process online at http://www.irs.gov.

Having employees carries other responsibilities and legalities with it. To begin with, you will need to pay payroll taxes (otherwise known as "withholding") to cover income tax, unemployment insurance, Social Security, and Medicare, as well as file W-2 and W-4 forms with the government. You will also be required to pay worker's compensation insurance, and will probably also want to find medical insurance. You are also required to abide by your state's nondiscrimination laws. Most states require you to post nondiscrimination and compensation notices in a public area.

Many employers are tempted to unofficially hire workers "off the books." This can have advantages, but can also mean entering a legal gray area. (Note, however, this is different from hiring freelancers, a temp employed by another company, or having a self-employed professional such as an accountant or bookkeeper come in occasionally to provide a service.) It is one thing to hire the neighbor's teenage son on a one-time basis to help you move some boxes, but quite another to have full-time workers working on a cash-and-carry basis. Regular wages must be noted in the accounts, and gaps may be questioned in the event of an audit. If the workers are injured on the job, you are not covered by worker's comp, and are thus vulnerable to lawsuits. If the workers you hired are not legal residents, you can also be liable for civil and criminal penalties. In general, it is best to keep your employees as above-board as possible.

Building a Business

Good business practices are essential to success. First off, do not overextend yourself. Be honest about what you can do and in what time frame. Secondly, be a responsible business owner. In general, if there is a problem, it is best to explain matters honestly to your clients than to leave them without word and wondering. In the former case, there is at least the possibility of salvaging your reputation and credibility.

Most business is still built by personal contacts and word of mouth. It is for this reason that maintaining your list of contacts is an essential practice. Even if a particular contact may not be useful at a particular moment, a future opportunity may present itself—or you may be able to send someone else to them. Networking, in other words, is as important when you are the boss as when you are looking for a job yourself. As the owner of a company, having a network means getting services on better terms, knowing where to go if you need help with a particular problem, or simply being in the right place at the right time to exploit an opportunity. Join professional organizations, the local Chamber of Commerce, clubs and community organizations, and learn to play golf. And remember—never burn a bridge.

Advertising is another way to build a business. Planning an ad campaign is not as difficult as you might think: You probably already know your media market and business community. The trick is applying it. Again, go with your instincts. If you never look twice at your local weekly, other people probably do not, either. If you are in a high-tourist area, though, local tourist maps might be a good way to leverage your marketing dollar. Ask other people in your area or market who have businesses similar to your own. Depending on your focus, you might want to consider everything from AM radio or local TV networks, to national trade publications, to hiring a PR firm for an all-out blitz. By thinking about these questions, you can spend your advertising dollars most effectively.

Nor should you underestimate the power of using the Internet to build your business. It is a very powerful tool for small businesses, potentially reaching vast numbers of people for relatively little outlay of money. Launching a Web site has become the modern equivalent of hanging out your shingle. Even if you are primarily a brick-and-mortar business, a Web presence can still be an invaluable tool—your store or offices will show up on Google searches, plus customers can find directions to visit you in person. Furthermore, the Internet offers the small-business owner many useful tools. Print and design services, order fulfillment, credit card processing, and networking—both personal and in terms of linking to other sites—are all available online. Web advertising can be useful, too, either by advertising on specialty sites that appeal to your audience, or by using services such as Google AdWords.

Amateurish print ads, TV commercials, and Web sites do not speak well of your business. Good media should be well-designed, well-edited, and well-put together. It need not, however, be expensive. Shop around and, again, use your network.

Flexibility is also important. "In general, a business must adapt to changing conditions, find new customers and find new products or services that customers need when the demand for their older products or services diminishes," says James Peck, a Long Island, New York, entrepreneur. In other words, if your original plan is not working out, or if demand falls, see if you can parlay your experience, skills, and physical plant into meeting other needs. People are not the only ones who can change their path in life; organizations can, too.

A Final Word

In business, as in other areas of life, the advice of more experienced people is essential. "I think it really takes three businesses until you know what you're doing," Drew Curtis confides. "I sure didn't know what I was doing the first time." Listen to what others have to say, no matter whether it is about your Web site or your business plan. One possible solution is seeking out a mentor, someone who has previously launched a successful venture in this field. In any case, before taking any step, ask as many people as many questions as you can. Good advice is invaluable.

Further Resources

American Independent Business Alliance

http://www.amiba.net

American Small Business League

http://www.asbl.com

IRS Small Business and Self-Employed One-Stop Resource

http://www.irs.gov/businesses/small/index.html

The Riley Guide: Steps in Starting Your Own Business

http://www.rileyguide.com/steps.html

Small Business Administration

http://www.sba.gov

Appendix B

Outfitting Yourself for Career Success

As you contemplate a career shift, the first component is to assess your interests. You need to figure out what makes you tick, since there is a far greater chance that you will enjoy and succeed in a career that taps into your passions, inclinations, natural abilities, and training. If you have a general idea of what your interests are, you at least know in which direction you want to travel. You may know you want to simply switch from one sort of nursing to another, or change your life entirely and pursue a dream you have always held. In this case, you can use a specific volume of The Field Guides to Finding a New Career to discover which position to target. If you are unsure of the direction you want to take, well, then the entire scope of the series is open to you! Browse through to see what appeals to you, and see if it matches with your experience and abilities.

The next step you should take is to make a list—do it once in writing—of the skills you have used in a position of responsibility that transfer to the field you are entering. People in charge of interviewing and hiring may well understand that the skills they are looking for in a new hire are used in other fields, but you must spell it out. Most job descriptions are partly a list of skills. Map your experience into that, and very early in your contacts with a prospective employer explicitly address how you acquired your relevant skills. Pick a relatively unimportant aspect of the job to be your ready answer for where you would look forward to learning within the organization, if this seems essentially correct. When you transfer into a field, softly acknowledge a weakness while relating your readiness to learn, but never lose sight of the value you offer both in your abilities and in the freshness of your perspective.

Energy and Experience

The second component in career-switching success is energy. When Jim Fulmer was 61, he found himself forced to close his piano-repair business. However, he was able to parlay his knowledge of music, pianos, and the musical instruments industry into another job as a sales representative for a large piano manufacturer, and quickly built up a clientele of musical-instrument retailers throughout the East Coast. Fulmer's experience highlights another essential lesson for career-changers: There are plenty of opportunities out there, but jobs will not come to you—especially the career-oriented, well-paying ones. You have to seek them out.

Jim Fulmer's case also illustrates another important point: Former training and experience can be a key to success. "Anyone who has to make a career change in any stage of life has to look at what skills they have acquired but may not be aware of," he says. After all, people can more easily change into careers similar to the ones they are leaving. Training and experience also let you enter with a greater level of seniority, provided you have the other necessary qualifications. For instance, a nurse who is already experienced with administering drugs and their benefits and drawbacks, and who is also graced with the personality and charisma to work with the public, can become a pharmaceutical company sales representative.

Unlock Your Network

The next step toward unlocking the perfect job is networking. The term may be overused, but the idea is as old as civilization. More than other animals, humans need one another. With the Internet and telephone, never in history has it been easier to form (or revive) these essential links. One does not have to gird oneself and attend reunion-type events (though for many this is a fine tactic)—but keep open to opportunities to meet people who may be friendly to you in your field. Ben Franklin understood the principle well—*Poor Richard's Almanac* is something of a treatise on the importance of cultivating what Franklin called "friendships" with benefactors. So follow in the steps of the founding fathers and make friends to get ahead. Remember: helping others feels good; it's often the receiving that gets a little tricky. If you know someone particularly well-connected in your field, consider tapping one or two less important connections first so that you make the most of the important one. As you proceed, keep your strengths foremost in your mind because the glue of commerce is mutual interest.

Eighty percent of job openings are *never advertised*, and, according to the U.S. Bureau of Labor statistics, more than half of all employees landed their jobs through networking. Using your personal contacts is far more efficient and effective than trusting your résumé to the Web. On the Web, an employer needs to sort through tens of thousands—or millions—of résumés. When you direct your application to one potential employer, you are directing your inquiry to one person who already knows you. The personal touch is everything: Human beings are social animals, programmed to "read" body language; we are naturally inclined to trust those we meet in person, or who our friends and coworkers have recommended. While Web sites can be useful (for looking through help-wanted ads, for instance), expecting employers to pick you out of the slush pile is as effective as throwing your résumé into a black hole.

Do not send your résumé out just to make yourself feel like you're doing something. The proper way to go about things is to employ discipline and order, and then to apply your charm. Begin your networking efforts by making a list of people you can talk to: colleagues, coworkers, and supervisors, people you have had working relationship with, people from church, athletic teams, political organizations, or other community groups, friends, and relatives. You can expand your networking opportunities by following the suggestions in each chapter of the volumes. Your goal here is not so much to land a job as to expand your possibilities and knowledge: Though the people on your list may not be in the position to help you themselves, they might know someone who is. Meeting with them might also help you understand traits that matter and skills that are valued in the field in which you are interested. Even if the person is a potential employer, it is best to phrase your request as if you were seeking information: "You might not be able to help me, but do you know someone I could talk to who could tell me more about what it is like to work in this field?" Being hungry gives one impression, being desperate quite another.

Keep in mind that networking is a two-way street. If you meet someone who has an opening that is not right for you, but you could recommend someone else, you have just added to your list two people who will be favorably disposed toward you in the future. Also, bear in mind that *you* can help people in *your* old field, thus adding to your own contacts list.

Networking is especially important to the self-employed or those who start their own businesses. Many people in this situation begin because they either recognize a potential market in a field that they are familiar with, or because full-time employment in this industry is no longer a possibility. Already being well-established in a field can help, but so can asking connections for potential work and generally making it known that you are ready, willing, and able to work. Working your professional connections, in many cases, is the *only* way to establish yourself. A freelancer's network, in many cases, is like a spider's web. The spider casts out many strands, since he or she never knows which one might land the next meal.

Dial-Up Help

In general, it is better to call contacts directly than to e-mail them. E-mails are easy for busy people to ignore or overlook, even if they do not mean to. Explain your situation as briefly as possible (see the discussion of the "elevator speech"), and ask if you could meet briefly, either at their office or at a neutral place such as a café. (Be sure that you pay the bill in such a situation—it is a way of showing you appreciate their time and effort.) If you get someone's voicemail, give your "elevator speech" and then say you will call back in a few days to follow up—and then do so. If you reach your contact directly and they are too busy to speak or meet with you, make a definite appointment to call back at a later date. Be persistent, but not annoying.

Once you have arranged a meeting, prep yourself. Look at industry publications both in print and online, as well as news reports (here, GoogleNews, which lets you search through online news reports, can be very handy). Having up-to-date information on industry trends shows that you are dedicated, knowledgeable, and focused. Having specific questions on employers and requests for suggestions will set you apart from the rest of the job-hunting pack. Knowing the score—for instance, asking about the value of one sort of certification instead of another—pegs you as an "insider," rather than a dilettante, someone whose name is worth remembering and passing along to a potential employer.

Finally, set the right mood. Here, a little self-hypnosis goes a long way: Look at yourself in the mirror, and tell yourself that you are an enthusiastic, committed professional. Mood affects confidence and performance. Discipline your mind so you keep your perspective and self-respect. Nobody wants to hire someone who comes across as insincere, tells a sob story, or is still in the doldrums of having lost their previous job. At the end of any networking meeting, ask for someone else who might be able to help you in your journey to finding a position in this field, either with information or a potential job opening.

Get a Lift

When you meet with a contact in person (as well as when you run into anyone by chance who may be able to help you), you need an "elevator speech" (so-named because it should be short enough to be delivered during an elevator ride from a ground level to a high floor). This is a summary in which, in less than two minutes, you give them a clear impression of who you are, where you come from, your experience and goals, and why you are on the path you are on. The motto above Plato's Academy holds true: Know Thyself (this is where our Career Compasses and guides will help you). A long and rambling "elevator story" will get you nowhere. Furthermore, be positive: Neither a sad-sack story nor a tirade explaining how everything that went wrong in your old job is someone else's fault will get you anywhere. However, an honest explanation of a less-than-fortunate circumstance, such as a decline in business forcing an office closure, needing to change residence to a place where you are not qualified to work in order to further your spouse's career, or needing to work fewer hours in order to care for an ailing family member, is only honest.

An elevator speech should show 1) you know the business involved; 2) you know the company; 3) you are qualified (here, try to relate your education and work experience to the new situation); and 4) you are goal-oriented, dependable, and hardworking. Striking a balance is important; you want to sound eager, but not overeager. You also want to show a steady work experience, but not that you have been so narrowly focused that you cannot adjust. Most important is emphasizing what you can do for the company. You will be surprised how much information you can include in two minutes. Practice this speech in front of a mirror until you have the key points down perfectly. It should sound natural, and you should come across as friendly, confident, and assertive. Finally, remember eye contact! Good eye contact needs to be part of your presentation, as well as your everyday approach when meeting potential employers and leads.

Get Your Résumé Ready

Everyone knows what a résumé is, but how many of us have really thought about how to put one together? Perhaps no single part of the job search is subject to more anxiety—or myths and misunderstandings—than this 8 ½-by-11-inch sheet of paper.

On the one hand, it is perfectly all right for someone—especially in certain careers, such as academia—to have a résumé that is more than one page. On the other hand, you do not need to tell a future employer *everything*. Trim things down to the most relevant; for a 40-year-old to mention an internship from two decades ago is superfluous. Likewise, do not include irrelevant jobs, lest you seem like a professional career-changer.

Tailor your descriptions of your former employment to the particular position you are seeking. This is not to say you should lie, but do make your experience more appealing. If the job you're looking for involves supervising other people, say if you have done this in the past; if it involves specific knowledge or capabilities, mention that you possess these qualities. In general, try to make your past experience seem similar to what you are seeking.

The standard advice is to put your Job Objective at the heading of the résumé. An alternative to this is a Professional Summary, which some recruiters and employers prefer. The difference is that a Job Objective mentions the position you are seeking, whereas a Professional Summary mentions your background (e.g. "Objective: To find a position as a sales representative in agribusiness machinery" versus "Experienced sales representative; strengths include background in agribusiness, as well as building team dynamics and market expansion"). Of course, it is easy to come up with two or three versions of the same document for different audiences.

The body of the résumé of an experienced worker varies a lot more than it does at the beginning of your career. You need not put your education or your job experience first; rather, your résumé should emphasize your strengths. If you have a master's degree in a related field, that might want to go before your unrelated job experience. Conversely, if too much education will harm you, you might want to bury that under the section on professional presentations you have given that show how good you are at communicating. If you are currently enrolled in a course or other professional development, be sure to note this (as well as your date of expected graduation). A résumé is a study of blurs, highlights, and jewels. You blur everything you must in order to fit the description of your experience to the job posting. You highlight what is relevant from each and any of your positions worth mentioning. The jewels are the little headers and such—craft them, since they are what is seen first.

You may also want to include professional organizations, work-related achievements, and special abilities, such as your fluency in a foreign language. Also mention your computer software qualifications and capabilities, especially if you are looking for work in a technological field or if you are an older job-seeker who might be perceived as behind the technology curve. Including your interests or family information might or might not be a good idea—no one really cares about your bridge club, and in fact they might worry that your marathon training might take away from your work commitments, but, on the other hand, mentioning your golf handicap or three children might be a good idea if your potential employer is an avid golfer or is a family woman herself.

You can either include your references or simply note, "References available upon request." However, be sure to ask your references' permission to use their names and alert them to the fact that they may be contacted before you include them on your résumé! Be sure to include name, organization, phone number, and e-mail address for each contact.

Today, word processors make it easy to format your résumé. However, beware of prepackaged résumé "wizards"—they do not make you stand out in the crowd. Feel free to strike out on your own, but remember the most important thing in formatting a résumé is consistency. Unless you have a background in typography, do not get too fancy. Finally, be sure to have someone (or several people!) read your résumé over for you.

For more information on résumé writing, check out Web sites such as http://www.résumé.monster.com.

Craft Your Cover Letter

It is appropriate to include a cover letter with your résumé. A cover letter lets you convey extra information about yourself that does not fit or is not always appropriate in your résumé, such as why you are no longer working in your original field of employment. You can and should also mention the name of anyone who referred you to the job. You can go into some detail about the reason you are a great match, given the job description. Also address any questions that might be raised in the potential employer's mind (for instance, a gap in employment). Do not, however, ramble on. Your cover letter should stay focused on your goal: To offer a strong, positive impression of yourself and persuade the hiring manager that you are worth an interview. Your cover letter gives you a chance to stand out from the other applicants and sell yourself. In fact, according to a CareerBuilder. com survey, 23 percent of hiring managers say a candidate's ability to relate his or her experience to the job at hand is a top hiring consideration.

Even if you are not a great writer, you can still craft a positive yet concise cover letter in three paragraphs: An introduction containing the specifics of the job you are applying for; a summary of why you are a good fit for the position and what you can do for the company; and a closing with a request for an interview, contact information, and thanks. Remember to vary the structure and tone of your cover letter—do not begin every sentence with "I."

Ace Your Interview

In truth, your interview begins well before you arrive. Be sure to have read up well on the company and its industry. Use Web sites and magazines—http://www.hoovers.com offers free basic business information, and trade magazines deliver both information and a feel for the industries they cover. Also, do not neglect talking to people in your circle who might know about trends in the field. Leave enough time to digest the information so that you can give some independent thought to the company's history and prospects. You don't need to be an expert when you arrive to be interviewed; but you should be comfortable. The most important element of all is to be poised and relaxed during the interview itself. Preparation and practice can help a lot.

Be sure to develop well-thought-through answers to the following, typical interview openers and standard questions.

☞ Tell me about yourself. (Do not complain about how unsatisfied you were in your former career, but give a brief summary of your applicable background and interest in the particular job area.) If there is a basis to it, emphasize how much you love to work and how you are a team player.

☞ Why do you want this job? (Speak from the brain, and the heart—of course you want the money, but say a little here about what you find interesting about the field and the company's role in it.)

☞ What makes you a good hire? (Remember here to connect the company's needs and your skill set. Ultimately, your selling points probably come down to one thing: you will make your employer money. You want the prospective hirer to see that your skills are valuable not to the world in general but to this specific company's bottom line. What can you do for them?)

☞ What led you to leave your last job? (If you were fired, still try to say something positive, such as, "The business went through a challenging time, and some of the junior marketing people were let go.")

Practice answering these and other questions, and try to be genuinely positive about yourself, and patient with the process. Be secure but not cocky; don't be shy about forcing the focus now and then on positive contributions you have made in your working life—just be specific. As with the elevator speech, practice in front of the mirror.

A couple pleasantries are as natural a way as any to start the actual interview, but observe the interviewer closely for any cues to fall silent and formally begin. Answer directly; when in doubt, finish your phrase and look to the interviewer. Without taking command, you can always ask, "Is there more you would like to know?" Your attentiveness will convey respect. Let your personality show too—a positive attitude and a grounded sense of your abilities will go a long way to getting you considered. During the interview, keep your cell phone off and do not look at your watch. Toward the end of your meeting, you may be asked whether you have any questions. It is a good idea to have one or two in mind. A few examples follow:

☞ "What makes your company special in the field?"

☞ "What do you consider the hardest part of this position?"

☞ "Where are your greatest opportunities for growth?"

☞ "Do you know when you might need anything further from me?"

Leave discussion of terms for future conversations. Make a cordial, smooth exit.

Remember to Follow Up

Send a thank-you note. Employers surveyed by CareerBuilder.com in 2005 said it matters. About 15 percent said they would not hire someone who did not follow up with a thanks. And almost 33 percent would think less of a candidate. The form of the note does not much matter—if you know a manager's preference, use it. Otherwise, just be sure to follow up.

Winning an Offer

A job offer can feel like the culmination of a long and difficult struggle. So naturally, when you hear them, you may be tempted to jump at the offer. Don't. Once an employer wants you, he or she will usually give you a chance to consider the offer. This is the time to discuss terms of employment, such as vacation, overtime, and benefits. A little effort now can be well worth it in the future. Be sure to do a check of prevailing salaries for your field and area before signing on. Web sites for this include Payscale.com, Salary.com, and Salaryexpert.com. If you are thinking about asking for better or different terms from what the prospective employer offered, rest assured—that's how business gets done; and it may just burnish the positive impression you have already made.

Index